JANE
JACOBS
champion of cities,
champion of people

JANE JACOBS
champion of cities, champion of people

REBECCA PITTS

books for young readers

AN IMPRINT OF
Seven Stories Press

NEW YORK ▪ OAKLAND ▪ LONDON

A TRIANGLE SQUARE BOOK FOR YOUNG READERS
PUBLISHED BY SEVEN STORIES PRESS

Excerpt on page 154 from *Stamped: Racism, Antiracism, and You* by Jason Reynolds and Ibram X Kendi, copyright © 2020. Reprinted by permission of Little, Brown, an imprint of Hachette Book Group, Inc.

SEVEN STORIES PRESS
140 Watts Street
New York, NY 10013
www.sevenstories.com

College professors and high school and middle school teachers may order free examination copies of Seven Stories Press titles. Visit https://www.sevenstories.com/pg/resources-academics or email academic@sevenstories.com.

Library of Congress Cataloging-in-Publication Data

Names: Pitts, Rebecca, author.
Title: Jane Jacobs : champion of cities, champion of people / Rebecca Pitts.
Description: New York : Seven Stories Press, [2023] | Includes bibliographical references and index. | Audience: Ages 10-13 years | Audience: Grades 10-12
Identifiers: LCCN 2022058080 | ISBN 9781644212998 (trade paperback) | ISBN 9781644213001 (ebook)
Subjects: LCSH: Jacobs, Jane, 1916-2006--Juvenile literature. | City planners--Ontario--Toronto--Biography--Juvenile literature. | Women city planners--Ontario--Toronto--Biography--Juvenile literature. | Sociology, Urban--Juvenile literature.
Classification: LCC HT169.C22 T6675 2023 | DDC 307.1/216092 [B]--dc23/eng/20221208
LC record available at https://lccn.loc.gov/2022058080

Printed in the United States of America

2 4 6 8 9 7 5 3 1

CONTENTS

INTRODUCTION

"The thing that gives me the most hope about the
future is the young people. They don't know how
hard it is to make change, or to improve things,
and it's a good thing they don't know how hard it
is, because they have lots of energy and they often
have lots of idealism, and they work at it. By the time
they've gotten tired, and they know how much effort
it takes to move things a few inches, there's another
generation coming along. That's what gives me the
most hope. That sounds so banal, but I don't know
anything as hopeful as that."

—JANE JACOBS, age 84[1]

"I'm not all that different as far as I can see from when
I was thirteen years old."

—JANE JACOBS, age 77[2]

Jane Jacobs was a neighborhood organizer, a great disruptor, a public figure against the war in Vietnam, a
visionary writer, an observer of cities . . . and the list goes
on. She had *a lot* of reputations. Her book *The Death and
Life of Great American Cities* is required reading in many
urban planning classes throughout the world today—and it
was penned over a half century ago. Her ideas have inspired

international festivals and events, including Jane's Walk, a network of community-led public walking tours that happen in cities around the globe every spring.

So who exactly *was* Jane Jacobs? And why does her life's work still matter today? Born in Scranton, Pennsylvania, Jane came of age during the Great Depression and spent decades in New York City, where she rose through the ranks of the magazine world by writing about cities and what makes them work. Jane was a twentieth-century woman through and through.

She was also a brilliant community organizer. It's hard to read Jane's story and not be moved by the stunts she pulled. The relentless pressure she applied. The names she was called. How she unflinchingly led her community headfirst against the most powerful man in New York—and won. How she believed with her whole heart that ordinary people are the best equipped to reenvision their communities and reclaim them from a few men at the top.

And speaking of the men at the top: Jane spent years battling against the power-hungry advocates of so-called "slum" clearance and the construction of highways through the heart of her beloved city of New York. She more than earned her informal title of the "strategic mastermind" behind the nonviolent, people-led campaigns that defended her New York City neighborhood from destruction. She unwittingly cemented herself as a local hero.

Not *just* a fighter, Jane was *for* something too. She wasn't anti-housing or obsessed with keeping a neighborhood perfectly preserved, as if it was under glass. Instead, Jane organized alongside her neighbors to see to it that affordable, attainable housing was built in the West Village, where she lived for many years. Not way over there—in segregated neighborhoods far away from transit or jobs—but right *here*, on her street. Building public housing for people within the existing fabric of a community? Yes, she was definitely for that.

Jane Jacobs was a public intellectual too. She prized this aspect of her life's work above all else. The picketing and the public hearings and the scheming that she participated in were nuisances—they may have been necessary and unavoidable nuisances, but they got in the way. Jane considered herself a writer, an author, and a thinker first. But not the stuck-in-an-ivory tower kind of thinker. No. (She hated the whole business of college and all that it stood for.) Jane wrote for people who weren't professionals, academics, or experts.

Jane Jacobs's breakout book, *The Death and Life of Great American Cities,* was first published in 1961. It was an attack on—more like an evisceration of—city planning at the time. Conventional wisdom paid very little attention to the wants and needs of people who live in cities, Jane argued. City planning was a generous way of describing it. City destruction, it should have been called.

The reactions to Jane's book were polarizing. She was adored. But she was hated too. Her words have become

Jane Jacobs in 1969. ELLIOTT ERWITT/MAGNUM

gospel to some—and have been twisted by others to justify everything from the blocking of new housing in wealthy white communities to the creation of instant neighbor-hoods, which pop up seemingly overnight. (Jane would have referred to both of these as what they decidedly are: stale, uniform, and boring. *Death*.)

As we consider the impact and legacy of Jane's bestselling book, we will look at what she purposefully ignored: a thorough discussion of race and social divisions in her beloved city. Jane doesn't see (or doesn't choose to examine) why some people are excluded from accessing equal rights—from safety and comfort in public space, to education, to credit, to home ownership, to wealth building. She glosses over America's long history of racism and oppression embedded in our laws and systems. We'll explore, together, how this deliberate omission is the most significant and warranted criticism of Jane Jacobs's work.

It is my hope that you—truthseekers—will engage actively with Jane's story. Jane was a strategic thinker who tipped the scales of power, winning civic battles through nonviolent direct action. Her legacy is also one that requires a thoughtful, critical examination.

Young people like you understand that we are each the expert of our own lived experiences. It is your generation, after all, who will reenvision our cities and places. And this must happen in the face of our looming climate crisis, all while grappling with America's history of racist policies and laws that still inform everything from where people live, to what schools and jobs are available, to access to the voting booth, to how people are policed.

Whew.

It's a lot to consider, but there is much to be hopeful about.

At the beginning of her now famous book on cities, Jane tells us—her readers—that we won't find a single illustration within the pages of *Death and Life*. Instead, the illustrations are out *there*, in the real world.

So go on—get out there on the street and have a look, she writes.

And "while you are looking, you might as well also listen, linger, and think about what you see."[3]

I hope you'll take Jane's approach as you engage with her work and life story.

That you'll cheer on, reject, admire, be wowed by—and question—Jane.

NOTE: This is a true story. Occasionally, I use invented dialogue to move the narrative along. (Anything conversational in italics is adapted or simplified from actual quotes, but the essence is based in facts and historical evidence. Anything in quotation marks is a direct quote from Jane herself.)

PHILADELPHIA, 1955

When Jane Jacobs arrived in Philly on assignment as a
reporter, she was feeling really good about the way things
were going. For her. For progress. For the future.

The magazine *Architectural Forum* sent her, and she was
happy to go. The story would be straightforward—just like
all the other ones. Stories of a metropolis reborn. Of the
men in charge, the planners, and their modern vision of a
successful city. Homes over here. Shops over there. Everything connected by superhighways.

But somewhere in the middle of it all—in the middle of
nothing, to be more specific, in the vast stretches of space
between towering housing projects—things, well, started to
look less clear. Muddled.

She might even go as far to say it was falling apart: the story
that she, along with what seemed like everyone else, had bought.

This is the good neighborhood, the planners told her.
Looming, massive buildings punctuated a great wide
park—empty except for a single boy kicking a tire.[1]

And this is a bad neighborhood, they said, as they toured
the area of town that was next to go. But all she saw was
a bustling Black community. An ordinary city scene of
people coming and going. She saw people on errands, families on stoops beside playing children.

Jane was there as an observer, covering the so-called "slums" of Philly. The word "slum" wasn't just a derogatory and racist label—although it definitely *was* that. It was also a legal designation used by the men who were in favor of a new kind of city. This process had a name, and it was "urban renewal"—a term that painted a picture of an eternal spring in the heart of the city. Urban renewal started with the false idea that the city was dirty and wretched, and—get this—that it had to be "saved" by the people in offices who make plans for the way things should be.

And by "saved"—well, what that really meant was that these places would first need to be torn down.

The people who lived there? They were collateral damage who could be paid off. Cash gets people packing their bags. But before the builders could send these people packing, destroy their neighborhoods, and build their new cityscape, completely disconnected from what (and who) was there before—these urban renewal guys had to prove that these places were disgusting and dangerous.

They had to paint the picture of the story they were peddling.

Oh, they had pretty statistics and charts of data to back up whatever they said.

And yeah, they had an answer for every question.

Except one.

What's to come of a place that's been completely erased? Jane asked them. *How is this good?*

CHAPTER 1

GROWING UP JANE

The moon, with all her brilliant light
Illumines only space and night.
The stars with but each other's aid
Stand clearly out, all unafraid.
Without a light to help explore,
Some things seem clearer than before.

—"To a Teacher," a poem by young Jane Butzner[1]

It was a perfectly average weekday morning in Scranton, Pennsylvania—at the time, a booming small city, which young Jane Butzner and her family called home. But unlike the rest of her classmates, Jane was not in school.

She had been expelled from third grade—sent home in the middle of the day.

Another child might have sat down in the schoolyard and cried. Waiting for the end-of-day bell to ring, wiping her face of any evidence of tears.

Instead, Jane pushed open the doors to the world outside textbooks and rules, memorization, and conformity.

Freedom.

Jane's mind raced. Should she rush home and apologize to her mom? Try to defend herself? She picked up her pace, heading toward the train tracks, past the area where the children were told to never go. She scaled the rocks, feeling a new rush of independence.

She was just seven years old, and for the first time in her life, she tasted what it felt like to stand one's ground, completely alone and apart from everyone else.

It was her first act of rebellion—in a long line of rebellious acts to come.

* * *

So why exactly *did* Jane get kicked out of school?

It just so happened that the very night before Jane's expulsion, her father had pulled her aside to dole out one of his lessons. He always had some idea or tidbit for his children that they *just had to know*. Usually there was a moral lesson tucked in there—the more philosophical, the better.

"Never promise to do anything for the rest of your life while you're still a child," he told her. "Promises are serious."

Would you believe that the very next morning at school, Jane's teacher asked every child in the classroom to raise a hand and promise to never miss a day of brushing their teeth?

Suddenly, school was interesting. Jane probably even forgot about the book she was secretly reading under her desk.

Instead, she watched with interest as all of the hands in class rose together.

All except for Jane's, that is. She not only refused to take that oath—she made the case to the other children that they, too, couldn't *really* be certain that they would keep their promise.

The teacher was incredulous. It was one thing to refuse. It was another to encourage resistance in others. She couldn't believe that this seven-year-old had the nerve to defy her. Over teeth brushing, of all things.

The teacher pulled her aside to speak with her privately. She'd show her what happens to children who step out of line. *That's enough*, she said. *You can pack up your things and go home right now. You're expelled.*

* * *

Despite the dramatic early expulsion, those first few years of elementary school were mostly fun and interesting for Jane. She liked her teachers and learned a lot from them. But things changed quickly, and Jane grew increasingly bored. She had trouble listening and got a reputation as the kid who could get all the other children to laugh.

As an adult, Jane could make sense of her struggle to conform. To her, schools were places that kill creativity and independent thinking. And elementary school is where it all begins—where little kids are trained to be obedient.

She described herself during this period as mischievous at most—not particularly troublesome or destructive. (Jane was the girl making loud noises with paper bags in the lunchroom, a trick that would earn her a visit to the principal's office.)

Walking a fine line between rabble-rousing and respectful behavior, Jane seemed to relish finding out how far she could take things. Like all kids who act out, Jane demonstrated with her behavior that her needs were not being met in some part of her life. Junior high (and high school too) were admittedly awful places for Jane. Later in life, she wrote about the failures of school to meet the needs of adolescents. Teens and preteens find connection and worth through their relationships with others, by teaching younger children and authentically engaging in their community beyond the isolated, age-segregated walls of the American classroom.

When Jane was in eighth grade, she commuted from her small town to the city school in Scranton. A classmate later recalled how Jane would amuse her peers on their long lunch break. At the Scranton Dry Goods store, Jane went up the down escalator through crowds of people. Her friends stood by, both fearful and admiring of this girl who went her own way.

Someone who worked in the store was mad all right—but nothing really happened. It was almost as if Jane was testing—in a really immature way, sure—what it felt like to disrupt the so-called norm.

It turned out that she delighted in it.

* * *

But back to getting kicked out of school.

All of the outdoor play had made Jane hungry, so she wandered home for lunch. Really, Jane had planned on telling her mom what happened, but the two of them ended up saying little to each other during the meal.

By the time her belly was full, she had decided. She knew what she had to do.

She'd go right back to school.

What would happen? What would her teacher say? Jane wasn't sure what to expect when she walked back through that door.

But there she went, back to her desk where she belonged. The whole thing was stressful for Jane, but it solidified a new kind of self-awareness—an antiauthoritarian streak she could not stifle or ignore.

"If I were running a school," Jane shared later in life, "I'd have one standing assignment that would begin in the first grade and go on all through school, every week: that each child should bring in something said by an authority—it could be the teacher, or something they see in print, but something that they don't agree with—and refute it."

As Jane took her seat in the middle of lessons, no one said a word. Knowing Jane, she probably pretended to listen before discreetly reaching into her desk for the book she preferred to whatever lesson was currently underway. Her eyes went back to what *she* wanted to know—to what *she* thought was interesting.

Without incident, the lessons continued.

Jane's school day dragged on, just like every other day. It was almost as if nothing had ever happened at all.

* * *

The thirteen-year-old riding the escalator in the wrong direction, the seven-year-old taking a stand—you might think that Jane Jacobs came from a long line of outspoken, offbeat adults. But Jane Jacobs's childhood looked like that of the typical American upper-middle-class white Protestant suburban family in the 1920s.

When it came to their principles and values, however, the Butzners were anything but conforming or conservative. "I was taught that the American's right to be a free individual, not at the mercy of the state, was hard-won," she wrote as an adult. Americans had fought for her freedom to speak her mind, even when her ideas went against popular opinion or the government. Jane's parents also taught her that with this freedom comes the job of "eternal vigilance" against threats to one's civil liberties. "I too would have to be vigilant," she wrote. "I was made to feel that it would be a disgrace to me, as an individual, if I should not value or should give up rights that were dearly bought."

* * *

Jane Jacobs was born Jane Isabel Butzner on May 4, 1916. For the first few years of her life, north Scranton was home to Jane, her sister, and her two brothers. (She had a fourth sibling—an older brother—who died young.) When Jane was four, they moved to 1712 Monroe Avenue in Dunmore, a nearby suburb in the heart of coal country.

Jane's father, John Decker Butzner (who went by "Decker"), was a prominent Scranton physician. He was working in a hospital in Philadelphia when he met Jane's mother, Bess Robison Butzner, a night nurse who had also worked as a schoolteacher.

In Jane's family, women worked outside the home. Most of them were schoolteachers like Jane's mother. While the women in her family held traditionally female professions, Jane grew up with the idea that women could do anything they set their mind to. "I was treated much the same as my brothers," she said.

It was a great gift that was unusual for its time.

Jane might not have realized it then, but she surely must have felt the importance of her upbringing later on in life. From the perch of old age, Jane recalled her formative years with her father, who was not only devoted to her but fiercely committed to stoking her intellectual curiosity.

"What's the purpose of life?" young Jane asked her father one evening, during one of their discussions together.

It was a simple question with no easy answer.

"Look at that oak tree. It's alive," her father said. "What's *its* purpose?"

Jane kept thinking. She was wondering the same thing people spend their whole lives wondering about.

What is the oak tree's purpose? What is mine?

It is simply to live, she decided.

* * *

John Butzner had a purpose in life, and, as far as professions go, it was an important one. He was a doctor, and his path to that career began humbly as a farm boy.

In the 1880s in Virginia, there weren't public schools for children. The options for education were pretty limited, especially if there was a farm to take care of. A young woman, usually a cousin, served as a teacher for all of the farm boys in Jane's father's extended family. They'd gather weekly for their lessons, and when the teacher married and moved on, another would take her place.

With only one year in an official school, Jane's father attended the University of Virginia on a family member's investment, a small fortune of $5,000 that sent him and all of his cousins to college. He was part of the first generation in the United States since the Civil War to attend college and went as far as one could go in schooling—all the way to earning his medical degree.

* * *

Jane's mother, Bess, was born in 1879. She grew up in the small town of Espy, Pennsylvania. Espy was important because it was centrally situated for getting coal to the Baltimore area. Bess's father—Jane's grandfather—had been a captain in the Civil War, fighting to end the American institution of slavery and keep the country together.

Bess and Jane kept up a correspondence until Bess passed away in 1981, when Jane was sixty-three years old. Their letters covered everything from the absurdity of what was happening with the American government, to local news, to notes of a proud mother describing her children's work, to the everyday details of whatever happened to be blooming in the family garden.

These handwritten notes are windows to the world of what stirred Jane. But more significantly, they are mirrors of their love for one another—mother and daughter, devoted and bonded for life.

* * *

Decker's lesson on morals prompted Jane to disrupt class. It was hardly a one-off teaching moment: Jane's parents told their children that they did not always have to accept or believe what someone in a position of authority says.

"I was brought up to believe that there is no virtue in conforming meekly to the dominant opinion of the moment," she wrote.

With nonconformist parents, Jane was free to entertain the eccentricities she developed in childhood. They were at the very least accepted, if not outright encouraged.

One of these quirks was having ongoing imaginary conversations with the politician and inventor Benjamin Franklin. "He asks very good questions," Jane later said of her make-believe friend. "Obviously, he's fascinated if I'm walking along the street. He's rather shocked with the way women are dressed, but he gets used to it. I explain how traffic lights work. On a trip to the subway, we stand on the platform and he's interested in the system of depositing used newspapers here and other litter there."

You could call it a strange pastime, to go about one's day ruminating to a dead historical figure on mundane matters that we all take for granted. Odd as this was, it was clear that Jane needed an outlet to make sense of her ideas. She had so many thoughts and observations about the world around her that she projected these ideas onto fixed historical characters, who served as a kind of filter for her own understanding of her environment. She also talked to an imaginary Thomas Jefferson, but Jefferson grew bored of her musings on how ordinary, everyday things work.

Franklin, however, was her perfect match. "Like Jefferson, he was interested in lofty things, but also in nitty-gritty, down-to-earth details," Jane recalled, "such as why the alley we were walking through wasn't paved, and who would pave it if it were paved. He was interested in everything, so he was a very satisfying companion."

* * *

What was life like in Pennsylvania for young Jane? Jane's family surely enjoyed a slice of the American dream in Dunmore, with the beauty and nature of the Pocono Mountain lakes and streams just beyond their small town. Monroe Avenue was a tree-lined road with sidewalks and large, ornate Victorian houses, and the Butzners' family home was roomy and comfortable.

In the 1920s, the coal business was doing well. Really well. Immigrants from Italy and Eastern Europe were the latest wave of newcomers to take on the dangerous work of coal mining. Wives of the men in the coal mines wove silk fabric and clothing, developing a bustling textile industry alongside the mining of anthracite coal.

Jane experienced—and noted, perhaps even out loud to Mr. Franklin—what it was like to live in a thriving city with access to great schools, the theater, public libraries, colleges, churches, and parks. With a population of one hundred thirty thousand people around the time Jane was born, Scranton had earned the futurist name "Electric City" for its streetcar system, the third largest in the US at the time.

But Scranton's story is one that is familiar to all too many places—it is a town that became too focused on just one thing. Even before the Great Depression took hold, Jane's family saw firsthand how economic decline can happen in a city. Anthracite coal, or superior coal, was Scranton's great resource, and there were laws in place in America that prevented other kinds of coal from being sold. During World War I and after, these regulations were broken and forgotten. Scranton paid the price and Jane watched while the economy of her hometown diminished right before her eyes. And when that one thing disappeared, everyone felt the impact deeply. Later, Jane spoke about this in no uncertain terms. To Jane, her hometown was "a template of how a city stagnates and declines and may be part of the reason why that subject interested me so much, because I came from a city where that happened."

It might be expected that adult Jane could make these connections, after years of making observations about real, working economies of places. But Jane understood something fundamental about her hometown as early as the fourth grade, despite (or because of, given Jane's independent mind) her teacher's explanation of what created the great success story of Scranton.

Cities are built in places where there is water, said Jane's teachers.

This was true. Cities *were* generally built near places with access to a river or the ocean. Sure, there was a beautiful waterfall in Scranton. But was a rushing brook putting dinner on the table?

You can almost hear Jane's imaginary conversation on her walk home from school. Once she was out of earshot of the other children, she'd say to Mr. Franklin, *I have my doubts about the waterfall.*

Go on . . . he would say.

It's a lovely thing, all right, but it's not the reason for Scranton's success today.

Ben was interested now. *What's that, then?*

Mines are the thing here, she'd say. *And the nice story about the pretty stuff just glosses over the obvious thing, the actual thing that employs people and pays for food. The real thing that makes a place work.*

* * *

Jane enjoyed the independence of mobility she experienced in her childhood. Children walked and biked around their neighborhoods to get around. It was the culture. It was what people did. Her father was one of the first doctors in town to get a car, a little red convertible. Its headlights were gas lamps and it lacked a windshield. Jane described the car as a tool just like any of the devices that would fit in her father's doctor's kit. But the car was not for them to use whenever it suited them, and her parents were certainly not her chauffeur. If Jane could get a ride someplace because her parents were going there anyway, she'd take it. More often than not, however, she'd hop on the streetcar to get downtown.

Driving was not part of their daily life—nor anyone's, really. Jane was living in a time and place that was beginning to modernize—with advancements in technology and transportation like the electric streetcar and motorcar—before the drastic impact that the automobile had on the US later in the twentieth century.

The car came in handy for big trips, though. The Butzners piled into the "roadster" to visit relatives in Virginia, and to see the sights in Washington, DC, at a time when there were sheep on the front lawn of the White House. Jane and her family drove to New York City when Jane was just twelve years old. It was a formative trip for Jane, one that stoked a lifelong interest in a city like none she had ever seen before.

Jane's parents instilled in their children an appreciation and respect for the big city. "They thought the cities were far superior places to live, and they told us why," Jane said.

When Jane stepped foot in Manhattan in 1928, it was beyond what she had imagined of the storied place. Wealthy people were experiencing an economic boom. They had extra cash to spend on *stuff*—the latest fashions and new conveniences. The big financial crash that was coming (and, boy, was it coming) hadn't yet happened.

It was lunchtime on Wall Street and the city was alive.

People were *swirling*. Going places, living in this big, magical experiment of collective energy and anonymity. A million stories in three hundred square miles.

And Jane was simply flabbergasted at the sight of it.

* * *

Later, Jane would become known for her magazine articles and books about cities. Did she begin to observe and collect her ideas on that significant first visit to New York? Perhaps. But it wasn't skyscrapers or shopkeepers that inspired her first published piece in a national magazine. Her subject centered on something far more familiar to her than America's most bustling metropolis.

Jane was an avid reader who loved writing poetry. She loved the feeling of stringing words together. At the young age of nine, she was a published poet in the local newspaper.

That early success likely fueled her drive to go bigger. In 1927, she shared her work by submitting it to the Girl Scouts' magazine, *American Girl*. To her delight, her poem about the experience of walking in nature under the pitter-patter of rain was accepted! And so it began: the thrill of seeing her name and ideas in print, out there for everyone, across the whole country, to see.

Did Jane realize then that there was nothing else like that feeling?

Maybe. It was certainly the start of what would become a lifelong conversation.

Except these weren't private chats with historical figures on the paths and sidewalks of Dunmore. These were conversations between Jane and her readers, conversations that everyone could see and interact with and think about.

This was eleven-year-old Jane, stepping out.

* * *

The 1920s marked a new chapter for social and political progress: the decades of work by suffragists brought women the right to vote with the ratification of the Nineteenth Amendment in 1919. (Practically, this meant that white women could now vote. For people of any gender who weren't white, access to these same rights wouldn't come until much later, with the passing of the Voting Rights Act of 1965.)

In a short period of time, some women made great strides, gaining more rights and access to different opportunities. Jane surely felt the changing tide of attitudes toward women and girls. "I grew up with the idea that I could do anything. Nothing was going to be barred from me if I wanted [it]."

Because of World War I, many more women were

employed, working in new weapons factories or filling empty jobs left by men who were off fighting. In fact, about 25 percent more women held jobs.

But it was still very much a man's world, as these were typically low-wage jobs, and many women saw no chance of working outside the home.

It wasn't as if Jane was naïve or unaware of gender inequality. She recognized that men still held more power than women. She detested this fact of life, even.

And yet—she still felt she could do anything.

She made the choice not to dwell too long on whatever women weren't allowed to do. She'd rather just go out and do it, even if she wasn't supposed to.

Especially if she wasn't supposed to.

* * *

There were dreams of poetry and writing, and then there were the practicalities of life that had to be considered. Jane's parents could have said that writing was simply not an option. (Knowing Jane, she might have forged ahead anyway.) Instead, they insisted that all of their children— not just their sons—explore their dream careers while also making a backup plan for earning income.

By the time she graduated high school, Jane knew that she was simply done with school. She had zero interest in college. She knew herself well enough then to know that it wasn't for her. While her parents encouraged her to go, they accepted her decision.

What she really wanted to do was get a job as a writer or a reporter at a newspaper. However, with limited options as a young woman just starting out, she instead enrolled in a trade school to learn stenography, a skill that involves using a specialized machine that allows notetakers to type very quickly. It would prove very useful in the coming years. "If I do say so myself, I became a good stenographer," Jane later shared. "I am very glad I did, for I earned my living with it—and thus in a sense my independence—for many years."

* * *

But before Jane fell back on this useful skill, she got a taste of the career that was her life's calling: writing.

She took a job reporting and writing for a Scranton newspaper. Her "beat"—meaning the type of story she was usually assigned—was what was then known as women's issues and interests. She'd write about weddings, parties, church suppers, and volunteer committees. Did Jane have a burning curiosity to cover these stories? No, but she approached them with the same upbeat attitude and willingness to take on assignments that characterized her approach to her writing work throughout her lifetime, drawing her closer and closer to the work she really wanted to be doing.

According to a friend's retelling of this period in her life, Jane started an advice column for the paper—then called an "agony column"—to advise readers on personal matters. Jane, faced with the problem of not having a single letter seeking her wisdom, faked a letter from a person requesting help so she had something to respond to.

She then proceeded, in subsequent issues, to call herself out on distributing such awful advice.

The paper piled on more and more responsibility. Soon enough, Jane was reporting and writing on her own ideas for newsworthy stories.

As a high school graduate without a single day in a college class, Jane was lucky to be doing exactly the work she wanted to be doing—during a time of extreme economic hardship.

Of course, her luck was running out, fast. America was years into the devastating period known as the Great Depression. The country was undergoing a painful transformation that was entirely out of her control.

* * *

Jane was thirteen in 1929 when the Great Depression hit, shattering the stretch of American prosperity known as the Roaring Twenties. The stock market crashed. People panicked and pulled their money out of banks. The banks, in turn, bottomed out. Unemployment skyrocketed. Businesses shuttered. Many people lost their homes and their jobs. Some lived in communities of shacks called "Hoovervilles," named after Herbert Hoover, the president at the time.

Jane's long-term job prospects in Scranton were slim, even with real reporting experience. After a year at the newspaper, Jane knew that she had no real future there. It was time for her to move on.

New York was the big city that loomed large in her imagination—and the possibilities for finding work there were probably better than anywhere else.

Jane's parents wanted her to experience life beyond her small suburban world. But it wasn't New York they were thinking of. They wanted Jane to move to the South.

Jane agreed, perhaps begrudgingly at the time.

In 1934, at the age of eighteen, Jane arrived in the western part of North Carolina, in a town called Higgins, framed by majestic rolling mountains blanketed in mist.

She stayed with her aunt Martha Robison, who was running a community center for the Presbyterian home missions. (Home missions are groups of people who organize to promote their religion locally as opposed to abroad. Missionaries also provided essential services like food distribution, health care, and education.) In the rural, impoverished countryside in Higgins, the Great Depression hit hard, and people were suffering. They had already been struggling well before that—since the end of the First World War.

Farmers had overproduced during wartime and couldn't

sell all their crops of cotton, wheat, and corn. They had also taken on too much debt and were saddled with costly equipment that wasn't giving them the return on investment envisioned during the boom times. They couldn't even afford to transport their goods to the market—so while food rotted in the country, people went hungry across America.

Rural areas are dependent on other, bigger places—cities. Jane's six-month stay in Appalachia provided yet another backdrop to her thinking on how places thrive or become stagnant—the ideas that would form the foundation of her life's work. It was an experience that remained with her, always.

In an autobiography she wrote for *Architect's Journal* in 1961, Jane expressed gratitude to her parents for sending her to Appalachia as a young woman. She was glad for the experience, as much as she was glad for the opportunity to begin her own life elsewhere, in a place where her odds for success were much higher.

That place, of course, was New York City.

CHAPTER 2

WHAT *IS* THIS PLACE? (CHRISTOPHER STREET)

"The stretch of Hudson Street where I live is each day the scene of an intricate sidewalk ballet. . . . When I get home after work, the ballet is reaching its crescendo. This is the time of roller skates and stilts and tricycles, and games in the lee of the stoop with bottle tops and plastic cowboys; this is the time of bundles and packages, zigzagging from the drugstore to the fruit stand and back over to the butcher's; this is the time when teenagers, all dressed up, are pausing to ask if their slips show or their collars look right; this is the time when beautiful girls get out of the MG's; this is the time when the fire engines go through; this is the time when anybody you know around Hudson Street will go by."

—JANE JACOBS[1]

When Jane moved to New York City in 1934, it wasn't as if she was a complete stranger in a new land. Betty, Jane's older sister, was already living in Brooklyn on Orange Street, in the picturesque neighborhood of Brooklyn Heights, situated across the East River with views of downtown Manhattan and the Statue of Liberty. Jane moved right into her sister's apartment, saving them both some money on rent. They were the kind of sisters who got along, enjoying each other's company. Which was a good thing, because their living space on the top floor of their six-story walk-up was tiny, even for a New York apartment. (The building where Jane's New York City story began is no longer standing: it was later torn down to make way for a highway.)

New York wasn't the same as Jane remembered, though. Gone was the city she'd visited during the heyday of the Roaring Twenties. Now, unhoused and unemployed people filled the streets. People were struggling to pay for food and shelter.

Jane was determined to find a job, and not just any job—she still wanted to write for a newspaper or magazine. However, she quickly realized that she would have to adjust her expectations: "Finding any kind of job was a great coup as I soon discovered." Every morning, Jane would scan the paper to see which employment agencies had placed ads, then she would set out on foot to introduce herself in person.

It felt like an impossible task, though. Poverty, house-lessness, and unemployment were everyday realities for Americans throughout the 1930s. By 1933, around 25 to 30 percent of Americans couldn't find work.

Even with President Franklin D. Roosevelt's New Deal, the sweeping plan intended to get the economy going and provide relief to some of those who were suffering, it was still extremely challenging for Jane to get hired. She was a nineteen-year-old woman without a college degree.

Each day, as Jane walked across the Brooklyn Bridge into Manhattan in search of work, she heard the same story, over and over again.

Nope.

Nothing here.

No one was hiring.

* * *

Her free time was both a curse and a blessing. Jane knew nothing about the city and was hungry to understand it and experience it. In the afternoons after job hunting, she would spend a nickel to ride the subway, picking stops at random to explore. It was on one of these unplanned excursions that Jane stumbled on the neighborhood that would become her home for decades.

"Betty, I found out where we have to live!" Jane said to her sister after one of these trips.

Betty wanted to know where this dream place was, exactly.

"I don't know," Jane replied, "but you get in the subway and you get out at a place called Christopher Street." (She had first chosen the stop because she liked the sound of its name.)

Jane didn't know it then, but she had happened upon the New York neighborhood called the West Village, a bustling,

Christopher Street and Bleecker Street, 1936.
NEW YORK PUBLIC LIBRARY

diverse neighborhood filled with working-class families, bohemian artists, and young professionals.

It was comfortable and charming, full of "little streets" that she found pleasant. She had an intuitive sense that the place just felt right. "An area may be dilapidated, as this was," she said later, "but a certain person can sense its general social atmosphere, which may be hopeful and healthy. If it's a community, if it's stable, if people stay put, then you have a livable place."

"There's nothing like it and nowhere else I'd rather be," she told her sister.

* * *

They needed money before they could move though. Betty had a job, at least—she was working in a department store, Abraham & Strauss, in Brooklyn. But she, too, had had to settle. Even though she studied interior design in Philadelphia, she wasn't able to find fitting work.

Jane was relentless in her pursuit of a job—any job. And one morning, it happened. All of that research and footwork finally paid off. Jane Butzner was hired as a full-time secretary at a candy manufacturing company. OK, it wasn't a dream job. But Jane was employed.

With some income coming in, it was easy enough for Jane and Betty to find an apartment during the Great Depression. They knew exactly where to look too. They moved their belongings into an apartment on Morton Street near the Christopher Street subway stop in October 1935, about a year after Jane first arrived in New York. (Later on, they moved to Washington Place and in 1948 to Hudson Street.)

The Morton Street apartment was owned by a man named Oliver Williams, a real estate developer who talked about the value of the buildings in the West Village that other people easily overlooked. Jane found him to be kind, fair, and progressive. He was, perhaps, an influence on her later decision to invest in her beloved neighborhood.

In those early days of downtown living, Jane's favorite thing to do was stroll around and observe the collective rhythm and energy of her metropolis. She wanted to take it all in—the sights, smells, and people of this grand city. Children played on the sidewalk. Parents sat on stoops. Patrons spilled out of corner shops and cafés and bars and restaurants—it was a real community. The city streets surrounding her apartment were outfitted with every establishment and service any city-dweller might need. She walked the cobblestone streets alongside the low-hung iron fences and the three-story brownstone walk-ups, buildings that had been there for decades. "I just loved coming to New York," Jane said of her early days there. "New York was a place where you don't have to be big or important or rich or have a great plot of land or a great development scheme or something like that to do something. And maybe even do something new or something interesting. A place that has scope for all kinds of people."

* * *

Today, Greenwich Village is one of the most expensive and desired neighborhoods in New York City, but at that time, these same city blocks and buildings were considered run-down. In an interview toward the end of her life, Jane remembered how, when she first moved there in the 1930s, the entire area was called a "slum."

Jane and Betty couldn't afford to enjoy the city nightlife. Money was tight toward the end of the week, and the sisters would mix a powdered baby food called Pablum with milk in order to save money and stay nourished. It tasted awful, but they ate it. It was the most difficult period of Jane's entire life—she was adjusting to adult responsibilities during a period of extreme poverty and economic uncertainty.

The city was an exciting place, but it was overwhelming too. In the days before social media or texting, Jane and Betty would amuse themselves by playing a game they called "messages." How could two wildly dissimilar people (say, a headhunter in the Solomon Islands and a cobbler in Rock Island, Illinois) get a message to one another by word of mouth only? And who could do it with the fewest amount of people in the chain?

"I suppose we were trying," Jane later guessed, "in a dim way, to get a grip on the great, bewildering world into which we had come from our cocoon."

* * *

During those first five years in New York, Jane worked as a secretary for a steel distributor and for factories that made candy, clocks, and drapery hardware. The stenography skills she acquired as a teenager came in handy.

It seemed as if every time she secured a job, the company would shutter, leaving her unemployed again. Once she beat the company to the punch, quitting out of exasperation with her rote task of typing names and addresses on pink papers—each representing an order for a clock being sent out into the world. She was in the rat race, stuck in a pile of papers that she'd never get to the bottom of. And it was completely disheartening for her to make just a small dent in an endless duty that no one person could ever complete. "As you can see, I was very young and very impatient," she told an audience of young people many decades later.

Jane's nagging discomfort with the status quo likely served her well, however. During her frequent bouts of job hunting, Jane wandered her beloved city, observing everything, taking it all in. In the evenings, she'd process those thoughts at the manual typewriter, typing up her notes and observations from the day.

Writing fed her curiosity. Her daily practice transformed her relationship with her city. She began to understand things that were happening beyond the surface of appearances. She watched how the stuff of New York—the goods and products—moved from trucks to shop owners and into the hands of customers. She thought about the systems of commerce pulsing throughout the city and how the urban economy differed from her experiences in rural Appalachia.

In 1935, she began sending letters to magazines with ideas for articles. Days later, a big-name publication answered her pitch. They wanted to buy an article! *Vogue* magazine bought not only her essay on the fur market but also three others (covering the diamond, leather, and flower trades). The set of four stories would be published within the next two years. Amazingly, the pay she received for the four articles was equivalent to about three months of work as a secretary.

Jane was interested in everything. She wanted to know about the topics her teachers never got to in high school. Driven and insatiable, her desire for knowledge began to eclipse her distaste for formal education. She was changing, and felt she was finally ready to take her parents up on their long-standing offer to pay for college.

But it was around this same time that the Butzners suffered an immeasurable loss. Mr. Butzner died at the age of fifty-nine, one week after an emergency surgery. Jane's father—the man who encouraged his children to think for themselves without dictating to them how they should live their lives or what they should do with their days—was gone.

Her parents had always wanted Jane to go to college but they never forced it on her. And now, after the death of her father, Jane (the same person who hated school) entered Columbia University, testing the waters in courses here and there without applying to a particular degree program.

She was a student again.

* * *

Jane took courses in the General Studies program at Columbia, choosing subjects that fed her roving intellectual curiosity across disciplines—everything from geology and zoology to law, political science, and economics. (She passionately loved geology and zoology.) Jane was surprised to discover that she liked school. But her newfound interest wasn't enough to keep her there. For the second time in her life, Jane was kicked out of school. This time, it had nothing to do with promises, and had everything to do with her high school grades. They simply weren't good enough for Columbia.

The blow hit Jane hard, and she never returned to higher education. She harbored a distaste for the whole system and made a point of refusing to accept honorary degrees that were offered to her later in life.

They hadn't wanted her, and she didn't want them.

* * *

Who needs college when you have the whole city as your living, breathing university?

"Cities—how shall I put it?—they're the crux of so many different subjects, so many different puzzles," she later said. "If you get really interested in them—not necessarily just our ones now, but the ones that have been, too, you get in a very shortcut way into so many other subjects. There's almost nothing you can think of that cities don't provide some insight into. So wasn't it lucky to get interested in cities?"

Jane believed that the way to know the city was to walk the city. It was these on-the-ground experiences that provided the raw material for her first published writings on cities.

How did the Diamond District become the single block of shops through which all gemstones, at one point or another, pass? No one she interviewed for her *Vogue* article seemed to know, but "everything comes to the Bowery, if you wait long enough," one of the dealers told her as he explained the process by which jewelry is bought, sold, and bought again. Nearby, outside the pawn shops, "the lusty, tumultuous life of the Lower East Side" throbbed in "raucous chaos" while the 'El' roared on by. In these descriptions you can see her poetic wordplay at work—and her delight in the layered, complex urban ecosystem. She cast herself in the role of city naturalist.

Two years later, Jane published the last of the *Vogue* series, "Flowers Come to Town," describing how cut flowers arrive in a corner shop. First, they were harvested from regional farms and far-flung places like California and Canada. Then they traveled to New York harbors and delivery points by truck, boat, and plane. Jane described the similarity between the rich variety of the flowers and the diversity of the laborers and shopkeepers, immigrants from around the world who transported and sold floral arrangements, with dreams of one day becoming established shopkeepers themselves.

Through the lens of something as mundane as a flower

market, Jane got at the shared humanity of shopkeepers, men "who shyly admit that they are dottles for love, sentiment, and romance."

"Flowers" was a New York story through and through, highlighting the connection between the workers and the uptowners who purchased luxury items. And commerce was the thread connecting them all.

Jane's clever idea for breaking into the impenetrable magazine world of New York worked. On the surface, these were stories about the fashions of the day, topics that readers of women's magazines would be interested in learning more about. But at the same time, these were stories written with a sense of clarity and knowingness about urban life, Jane's true passion.

After the *Vogue* articles, she pitched ideas and landed Sunday feature stories at the *Herald Tribune* and *Cue* magazine. Although the money wasn't as good, she was gaining traction and getting paid to write.

"The lights of New York are the city's jewels," she wrote for an article in *Cue* magazine, "but her buttons and hooks and eyes are the squares and circles of metal that dot asphalt and sidewalks." Her essays were full of these kinds of wordy, delighted flourishes. She found joy and beauty in things as seemingly uninteresting as the network of cables and pipes below the sidewalks, what she called "underground spaghetti." These early writings reveal Jane's unwavering eye for observation, for unearthing the commonplace details of city life.

Sure, there were stars out there—somewhere behind the haze of the bright city lights. But it wasn't the sky that captured her attention in those first years in New York. Instead, she was absorbed in the world on the ground: the clanking garbage trucks with their 6:00 a.m. reign over the roadways. From her rooftop, looking down on her cherished neighborhood, she wondered in awe at the cycles and systems below. "What a complicated, great place this is," she thought, "and all of these pieces that make it work."

CHAPTER 3

FINDING LIFE'S FORTUNE

"You see, home is not just a building: it's a territory, the whole connection between you and other people and places."

—JANE JACOBS[1]

Jane Butzner was not going back to college. She knew this to be the simple, unbendable truth. But she was a secretary and she wanted to be a writer. Not a freelance writer who gets paid in dribs and drabs, but a full-time staff writer. How was she going to get *there* from here?

If she couldn't write for a magazine—yet—she'd work as a secretary *at* a magazine. In 1940, she was hired by *Iron Age*, a trade magazine about the iron and steel industry. Jane was inching toward the career she envisioned. "They hired me because I could spell molybdenum," she later shared, but it was more likely due to her genuine interest and budding talent in the journalism field. With a few freelance assignments under her belt, she quickly pivoted into a reporting and editorial staff position at the magazine.

In March 1943, in the midst of World War II, Jane used her position at *Iron Age* to point out a big problem in her hometown of Scranton, Pennsylvania. Too many men were unemployed and too many houses sat empty. (To be exact, thirty thousand men and seven thousand homes, according to Jane's research.)

She referred to the "strange neglect" of this town that had fought harder than any, according to her, to get jobs that would support the war. It was getting so bad that "in Scranton men are now applying for women's jobs," Jane reported. As Samuel Zipp and Nathan Storring, the editors of a book on Jane's writings, point out, the very opposite was happening in other parts of the country: women were filling the jobs left by men who were fighting in the war.

This article was a significant turning point for Jane. For the first time, she wrapped her arms around a story that was rooted in her own firsthand observations (with reporting to back it up) in order to bring attention to issues affecting the livelihoods, housing, and migration of families from her beloved hometown.

Jane was clearly beginning to flex her journalistic muscles, embracing the power of the media and using it as a vehicle for storytelling and attention. "The veins of anthracite coal [in Scranton] . . . are running out," she wrote, with a dramatic flair. Scranton had lost two-thirds of its mining jobs in the last decade, she explained. A commission appointed by the president himself was calling Scranton a hotbed of possibility for industrial production. War plants should be located there, wrote Jane.

Scranton was ready. They wanted the economic success their fellow Americans were experiencing. Residents made their case for more jobs in Washington. But the factories were blocked, again and again.

The responses from Washington were murky at best. "They provide a post-graduate course in the runaround," Jane wrote. DC couldn't even properly explain why Scranton was getting passed over.

Another reporter might have left it at that, but this was where Jane leaned in, cutting through the fluff and laying out the facts in what would become her signature style. Why was it that the state senator's office was claiming not to know why Scranton was being continually overlooked? The government first feigned ignorance. Then they became dismissive, claiming that Scranton was falling behind anyway. "What if they did get some war plants?" a secretary to the Pennsylvania senator told *Iron Age*. "It wouldn't help."

Later that year, an article *about* the article appeared in Jane's hometown paper, *The Scrantonian*. The town's pride for their "ex-Scranton girl" was palpable. According to the newspaper, Jane's story was picked up in over three hundred papers across the country. And it was the reason why the Murray Corporation chose to locate there to manufacture wings of warplanes, bringing thousands of new jobs to Scranton through the end of the war. Unfortunately, it wasn't the economic jolt that would transform Scranton. But Jane must have felt tremendous satisfaction at both the interest in her published article *and* the impact it had on the lives (and livelihoods) of real people.

*　*　*

Jane's professional life and personal life accelerated together, which is just another way of saying that Jane fell in love. Fast.

Jane met her future husband, the hospital architect Robert Hyde Jacobs Jr. (called "Bob"), in the spring of 1944 at a house party she threw with her sister and some friends. She had since moved on from *Iron Age* and was writing feature stories for the Office of War Information, an agency created by the president to spread information about World War II.

Bob was working at a defense plant with Jane's sister, Betty, who invited him to the gathering.

"I walked in the door," Bob later shared, "and there she was, in a beautiful green woolen evening dress, and I fell in love. It took me a little longer to convince her."

Hardly—Jane and Bob were married in May, just a month or so after they met. "The only reason we waited that long was so I could meet his parents," Jane reflected on their courtship. The story goes that Bob proposed to Jane just one week after meeting her. (Jane said no at first, but then changed her mind days later.)

Jane and Bob were married by a Presbyterian pastor at eleven in the morning on May 27, 1944, at her mother's home in Dunmore in a simple ceremony that was customary for the time. A few family members were in attendance for the ceremony and breakfast reception that followed.

After their honeymoon—a bicycle trip through northern New York State and Pennsylvania—Jane and Bob returned to New York to live at 82 Washington Place in the Village.

A few years later, they purchased a run-down, three-story brownstone at 555 Hudson Street in the Village. While another young, white couple might have been lured to the suburbs with the promise of a single-family home, Jane and Bob were invested in building a life in the city. They were kindred spirits both in personality and in values, with upbeat dispositions and a shared commitment to a path that was considered countercultural at the time.

They purchased the entire building for $7,000 and soon moved into their living quarters, above a candy shop and next door to a laundry service. A sea captain built it way back in the middle of the nineteenth century and it was—by the time the Jacobses bought it—the definition of a fixer-upper. Everything had to be redone, from the foundation to the interiors. Rats ran amok. The small plot of land out back was trashed. The neighborhood itself was noisy and full of clanking trucks. Jane and Bob tackled the house mostly by themselves, slowly renovating their home over

time and raising their three children in the heart of downtown Manhattan.

* * *

On the cusp of the 1950s heyday of white flight, when a lot
of white people were *leaving* the city in droves, the Jacobses
purchased their row house. Who lived in the West Village
then? Professionals like the Jacobses, laborers, unmarried
people, LGBTQ+ people, white people, Black people, people
who had migrated from Puerto Rico, immigrants, artists,
poets, musicians, families who could afford a down payment,
people who could barely afford rent and squeezed their
whole family in one crowded rented room. Jane and Bob
were a white middle-class couple who bought a fixer-upper
in a diverse, working-class neighborhood.

Let's pause here for a moment and introduce the word
"gentrification." In simple terms, it's this: new people move
in. They've got more money than existing residents. The
neighborhood changes, and the people who lived there
before can't afford it anymore, so they get pushed out.
Because of racist American laws—very much in place by
design, meant to uphold inequality—it's generally white
people with more money who are moving in and doing the
pushing out.

Gentrification is a word that comes up *a lot* when we talk
about Jane Jacobs, and rightfully so. She wrote about gen-

trification in her bestselling book but—a big but here—she missed some *really* important things about what causes it. If you charted the curve of gentrifying New York, Jane Jacobs was right there, in her home-improvement project amidst low (yet escalating) rents. And this is also true: Jane worked to prevent displacement—in all of its causes—by championing affordable housing in her neighborhood.

* * *

Before the rents were high, the Village was a place where artists and writers could create something without too many expectations made of them—either on their time or mental space. This freedom suited Jane. There were the glamorous caricatures of the city who passed her on the sidewalk, but Jane's experience of city life was far more mundane.

"People think living in Greenwich Village is terribly exotic in some way," Jane shared in her eighties, "but actually, you raise children, you make meals, you feel very good if you can get new curtains for your windows." She wasn't "in" with the bohemian crowd that flourished a bit later in the 1950s and '60s—larger-than-life characters like Bob Dylan and Dylan Thomas who cemented a place in Greenwich Village folklore. While Jane saw them on the street and in bars, she definitely didn't hang out with them.

One of the things Jane adored about living in the Village was the spontaneous interactions and connections that came along with living in close proximity with one's neighbors. Jane *wanted* the noisy bar on her street—to her, the local watering hole was an essential part of her community. There were functional benefits that came from having a popular outpost on her block. Patrons came in shifts: first the Irish longshoremen, then the literary cocktail party swooped in, continuing through the early morning hours. "On a cold winter's night, as you pass the White Horse and the doors open, a solid wave of conversation and animation surges out and hits you; very warming," she said. "The comings and goings from this bar do much to keep our street reasonably populated until three in the morning, and it is a street always safe to come home to."

* * *

Meeting Bob and having three healthy children together was one of Jane's greatest "achievements" in life. James Kedzie was born in 1948, Edward Decker in 1950, and Mary Hyde in 1955.

On the dedication page of *The Death and Life of Great American Cities*, she wrote:

> To New York City
> where I came to seek my fortune
> and found it by finding Bob, Jimmy, Ned and Mary
> for whom this book is written too

Did Jane come to New York to seek a different kind of fortune, in the way that young, driven, intelligent women do? Yes, she did. What is remarkable is that she managed to establish herself within her chosen profession while also raising a family. By 1940, around 28 percent of American women were employed out of the home. By 1945, largely due to women joining the workforce during World War II, around 34 percent held jobs. Today, it's not necessarily any easier to manage both a career and a family, but it doesn't come with the stigma that it once did. "In my generation, women were made to feel guilty if they didn't stay home and devote themselves to being wives and mothers," Jane told an interviewer in 1970. "If we worked at jobs or at a profession, we had to struggle against regarding ourselves as irresponsible, selfish, and willing to jeopardize the future."

But the great luck of her life was never lost on Jane. "Really, I've had a very easy life. I've spent most of it doing what I wanted to do. By 'easy' I don't mean just lying around; but I haven't been put upon really. And it's been luck mostly. Being brought up in a time when women weren't put down, that's luck. Finding the right man to marry, that's the best luck! Having nice children, healthy children, that's luck. All these lucky things."

* * *

By the time Jane was married, she had written and published a book. It wasn't *the* book—more on that to come. But it was *a* book, nonetheless. She never included it in her biography or listed it on her résumé as part of her body of work. This is likely because it had little to do with cities or economic theory. It had to do with the Constitution. It was a scholarly work with a quirky name, *Constitutional Chaff*. In it, Jane laid out rejected suggestions of the 1787 Constitutional Convention—an alternative Constitution that could have been.

Jane wrote the book while taking courses at Columbia and submitted a proposal to Columbia University Press, who liked the idea and agreed to publish it.

The writer Anthony Flint compared *Constitutional Chaff* to her later book on cities and found a connection. Sure, planners (of cities) and leaders (of governments) might lay the groundwork. But that's not enough, Jane argued.

To make something remarkable—something that can stand the test of time and better itself—that's up to the people themselves.

* * *

By the end of World War II, Nazis had killed six million Jewish people and millions of others (including disabled people, LGBTQ+ people, and people targeted for their race, political beliefs, or religion). The war ended like no other war has in the history of humanity, before or since. In 1945, the United States dropped atomic bombs on two Japanese cities, Hiroshima and Nagasaki, killing roughly one hundred fifty thousand people instantly. More would die of radiation poisoning.

Between 1942 and 1945, President Roosevelt issued a barbaric order to force Japanese Americans from their homes into incarceration camps. One hundred twenty thousand people of Japanese descent, most of whom were US citizens, were imprisoned.

Strikingly, even with these unprecedented acts of nuclear warfare and the obliteration of civil rights, most Americans were supportive of the war against the Axis powers of Japan, Italy, and Hitler's Nazi Germany.

When the war ended, Jane was laid off from her job at the Office of Wartime Information. She cobbled together freelance work for a full year before taking another job for the US government. Newly married, she was hired as a writer for the State Department and for the Overseas Information Agency's magazine *Amerika*, a publication for Russian readers that boasted about American sites and landmarks. Make no mistake, this was a glossy magazine pushing US propaganda.

Russia, America's ally in World War II, started to look more and more like the United States' enemy after the war ended. It was almost as if America's new leader in office, President Truman, wanted another war. Was this because war was good for the economy? Perhaps—it is a well-worn truth that corporations benefit from war. Whether it was economic motivation or irrational alarm, America's collective fear of Russia and the perceived threat of communism was growing.

In communism, a political theory laid out in Karl Marx and Friedrich Engels's *The Communist Manifesto*, all resources and property are communally owned instead of individually owned, and that wealth is redistributed back to all people. In the 1940s and '50s, the United States experienced a growing panic, stoked by elected officials, that communism was spreading throughout America and that Communists would soon overthrow the government. President Truman launched an investigation to uncover disloyal government employees. People lost their jobs and reputations, without a fair trial. This escalating mood of paranoia was referred to as the Red Scare, and Jane Jacobs found herself right in the middle of it.

One day, Jane discovered that she had landed on Joseph McCarthy's communist watchlist. Similar to Truman, the Wisconsin senator held trials against Americans for their communist beliefs and practices, either demonstrated or presumed.

McCarthyism was shorthand for the widespread, harmful way of thinking during this period in American history, when people were defamed or charged with crimes based on their political beliefs without any real evidence that they were committing treason against their country.

So how did Jane Jacobs discover that she was considered

a suspicious person by the United States government? In 1952, she received a letter from the US Department of State requiring her answers to their questions.

Incredulous, she followed up with a detailed response that included a lengthy foreword to the questionnaire "to put herself in context" for the government officials who were demanding an explanation from her.

It couldn't be that she had received such a letter because she was a member of the United Public Workers of America union or the American Labor Party, she wrote. No—it wasn't illegal in America to belong to those groups (you can almost imagine her saying this in a mocking tone). "I concluded," she went on, "that I am probably suspected of being a secret Communist Sympathizer or a person susceptible to Communist influence."

Jane was a believer in workers' rights and collective bargaining, and she joined the Workers of America union for this reason. She quickly understood that it was also operating as a communist political group. In her letter to the State Department, she defended her decision to remain a union member. When the union increasingly faced more scrutiny as a communist threat, Jane decided to stay on just to make a point: "The more a right is under attack, the more important it is to adhere to it, in principle."

But the interrogations were something that truly gave her pause. "It still shocks me," she writes in her letter, "although we should all be used to it by this time, to realize that Americans can be officially questioned on their union membership, political beliefs, reading matter, and the like. I do not like this, and I like still less the fear that arises from it."

In the years after 9/11 and America's overreaching and authoritarian Patriot Act, the humanitarian and activist Howard Zinn compared the fear of terrorism in the early 2000s to the perceived threat of communism in the middle of the twentieth century. During such times, ordinary people have a great responsibility to uphold our fundamental rights—including the right to free speech. "The recourse of citizens when civil liberties are attacked is first to expose those attacks as violations of basic freedoms guaranteed in the Bill of Rights; and second, to speak and write even more boldly than ever in order to encourage other people to do the same, so that the number of people speaking their minds becomes too great for the government to handle," Zinn said.[2]

To undermine the very backbone of the freedoms granted in the Constitution—the freedom to speak one's mind—was unacceptable to Jane, and she said so. She felt as though her right to live as a nonconformist was under attack, and she wouldn't apologize for the years she held membership in the union.

Soon after the State Department interrogated her via that letter, Jane resigned from her job at *Amerika*. She would never again work for the US government. Her early expressions of independence encouraged by her parents were coalescing into outright disgust of power that over-stepped its reach.

Jane felt that the right to criticize her government was the very essence of the American tradition. It is no luxury, she wrote in her letter to the State. "I do not agree with extremists of either the left or right, but I think they should be allowed to speak and to publish, both because they themselves have, and ought to have, rights, and because once their rights are gone, the rights of the rest of us are hardly safe."

CHAPTER 4

LOTS OF LIES

"When reason tells you one thing and the myth you were brought up with is at odds with it, the myth has to give—and that's not easy."

—JANE JACOBS[1]

Jane had burned her bridge with the State Department. That was fine with her; she didn't *want* a way back to government work.

But when you close one door, another one opens. All the clichés rang true.

In 1952, Jane began work at *Architectural Forum*, first as a reporter, and later as an associate editor. She was already an avid reader of the renowned magazine thanks to her architect husband Bob, who would leave it lying around at home. Now, instead of writing nationalist puff pieces, Jane would finally get to investigate and write about cities.

After a trial assignment, Jane was named the magazine's school and hospital expert. Rather than reveal to her bosses that she knew little about architecture or institutional design, she put in extra hours at home in the evenings over the course of those first few months, learning the industry she was supposed to be knowledgeable about. "I was utterly baffled at first, being supposed to make sense out of great, indigestible rolls of working drawings and plans," she wrote in 1962 in *Architect's Journal.*

Bob was a huge help, though. A graduate of Bard College and the Columbia School of Architecture, he held the credentials and had the professional experience that Jane did not. He was a great champion of her work and ideas, and was an especially invaluable asset during those early years when Jane was first writing about architecture in a professional capacity.

Together, they pored over architectural drawings. Slowly, bit by bit, she was becoming an expert.

* * *

Forum was a dream beat: she met with architects, city planners, and developers, and toured projects in cities *and* suburbs throughout the Northeast and Mid-Atlantic regions.

Many Americans were doing pretty well during this period in American history, wealth- and prosperity wise. But most people living in cities in the 1950s weren't the ones feeling the economic boom. Manufacturing jobs dried up, and poverty and unemployment swept in. Middle and upper class people, especially white people, were moving to the suburbs.

And coinciding with this flight to the suburbs was America's new love of the automobile. In 1954, the New York State Thruway opened, connecting New Yorkers to the suburbs and beyond. By 1956, President Eisenhower signed the Federal Aid Highway Act into law, marking the rapid growth of forty-one thousand miles of a massive interstate highway system.

"The great federal highway program now getting started will influence metropolitan land use for good or ill more than all the metropolitan land planning ventures of our time put together, but there is no sign that this is understood by those who wrote the legislation or those who will administer it," Jane wrote in the pages of *Architectural Forum* in 1957.

Over $2.5 billion would be spent in the coming decades threading US cities together in a network of high-speed roads. These fast new roads would transport products, goods, and military supplies much more quickly than ever before. They would also help people in the suburbs reach the city by car much more easily.

During this period of massive freeway development, car ownership became an American obsession, as did the uniquely American pastime of taking to the open road. The economic boom around war goods didn't just fizzle out when the war ended. Instead, a new kind of economy exploded: all the stuff that was getting made in the name of consumption and convenience. Suburban families had more money and they were buying up appliances and new goods they never knew they needed. The automobile industry paved the way with marketing schemes to match this growing market. In 1950, around 60 percent of families owned one car. By the end of the decade, car manufacturers were successfully selling the idea of the two-car family.

There is no doubt that America benefited economically from the great interstate highway system that began with Eisenhower's legislation. But is that the full story? What happened to those downtown neighborhoods that were ripped through, torn up, and bulldozed to create these superhighways? What were the downsides to developing a large-scale system of roadways? Were other options over-looked, like a greater investment in high-speed rail? What was lost—and who lost—in the process?

* * *

Along with an ever-expanding network of freeways and parkways, the population surged after the war. (Meet the baby boomers.)

Babies and suburbs go together like PB and J. More kids? In America, that means more house. The dream of the white picket fence.

Emphasis on white.

You see, this dream was obtainable for only one kind of family—white families.

The US government made it almost impossible for Black families and families of color to take part in the American dream of suburban homeownership.

In his book *The Color of Law*, Richard Rothstein traces the history of housing discrimination and redlining, the racist practice of refusing mortgages and home insurance based on race, ethnicity, or immigration status. The effects of these laws and policies have had long-lasting negative impacts on Black Americans in particular. "African Americans were unconstitutionally denied the means and the right to integration in middle-class neighborhoods, and because this denial was state sponsored, the nation is obligated to remedy it," Rothstein writes.[2]

So what exactly is "redlining"? Redlining is a term that comes from the areas of red that can be found on maps produced by the Home Owners' Loan Corporation (HOLC), a government-sponsored program created in 1933 to help homeowners who were struggling to pay for their home.

We have to go back to the Depression and the New Deal to understand the significance of these maps. With the New Deal, President Franklin D. Roosevelt was trying to jump-start the economy. In 1934, as a part of that series of programs, he addressed the housing crisis directly, passing the National Housing Act which in turn created the Federal

Housing Administration (FHA). Now, a new government agency, the FHA, was backing banks' loans—which meant that more and more mortgage loans were being issued.

Suddenly, people who could never have afforded a home were eligible to purchase one. FDR's vision for opening up homeownership to more people was a win-win. A whole bunch of construction jobs would be created too.

This all sounds good, right?

Well, it wasn't good for anyone who wasn't white.

HOLC created color-coded maps of neighborhoods in every major city across the nation. The neighborhoods highlighted in green were ranked the "best," meaning a large number of white businessmen lived there. The red portions of the maps marked "hazardous" areas—neighborhoods where "foreign-born people, low class whites, and negroes" lived, to use the language of the HOLC. Blue and yellow neighborhoods were flagged as somewhere in between. Other data were collected—but the presence of Black people, immigrants, and people of color was what made a neighborhood red. And living in a red area meant no mortgage and no loans.

And that wasn't all. If lenders, for whatever reason, even *thought* that people who fit this racial or ethnic background or citizenship status would begin moving into a neighborhood, well, that was enough for HOLC to say that the neighborhood was no good. The Federal Housing Administration produced a manual to help their assessors decide whom to grant guaranteed mortgages to. In Section 233, the manual states: "Investigate areas surrounding the location to determine whether or not incompatible racial and social groups are present, to the end that an intelligent prediction may be made regarding the possibility or probability of the location being invaded by such groups."

After World War II, the government helped veterans buy homes in the suburbs as a way of expressing gratitude for their service. Except this gratitude extended only to a few. Black veterans were denied mortgages, and many didn't even bother applying, knowing full well that they were not eligible. White families were able to get a head start on growing their wealth, and years later were able to pass that wealth on to their children.

President Truman, who became president in 1945 after Roosevelt's sudden death, did do some things to try to change the racism baked into America's DNA. In 1948, he ordered the armed forces to desegregate and, in 1954, the Supreme Court's historic ruling in *Brown v. Board of Education* did the same for the nation's schools. But segregation was still a reality, and Black people, immigrants, and people of color continued to be excluded from homeownership and "good" affordable housing. On top of not being able to obtain a mortgage, Black families faced yet another form of discrimination: some suburban homeowners would not sell homes to Black people at all.

So where did this leave the people who were shut out

of more resourced neighborhoods? What happened if you lived in the "red" zone?

The lasting impacts of redlining can still be felt today. In neighborhoods designated "hazardous," landlords stopped improving their properties. Housing conditions became unsafe. And because tax dollars fund education, the schools worsened too. Good jobs became scarce, so there were fewer opportunities for employment.

The trail of money flowed out of US cities—seemingly magically appearing like a gift in the pockets of white people who had moved to the suburbs.

* * *

Jane wrote as she had never written before. She was caught up in everything that was happening, thrilled by the idea of progress.

She had only good things to say about the strip mall projects that were bubbling up in the suburbs.

She also wrote with admiration about the huge, towering housing developments that were beginning to provide affordable homes to (some) people.

Gosh, isn't it great how the people in charge are considering everyone? she thought.

But the story of public housing was way more complicated than Jane's first impressions of it.

* * *

Public housing wasn't a brand-new concept when Jane began to first report on it. In 1937, as part of the New Deal, FDR passed the US Housing Act. This was huge: it marked the beginning of the federal government's involvement in public housing. "I see one-third of a nation ill-housed, ill-clad, ill-nourished," FDR said at his second inaugural address in 1937. "The test of our progress is not whether we add more to the abundance of those who have much; it is whether we provide enough for those who have too little."

Later that year, FDR passed a law that established the United States Housing Authority, which poured $500 million into affordable housing.

But was all public housing created equal? And who got to live in what kind?

The Public Works Administration, another New Deal program, funded segregated housing developments in cities across the nation throughout the 1930s. In *The Color of Law*, Rothstein argues that these sorts of projects accelerated segregation in American cities. In New York, for example, the Williamsburg Houses development only allowed white residents and the Harlem River Houses development was built for Black people.

After World War II, more public housing was built in New York City to house the middle class, and especially to house veterans. But so-called undesirable people—single parents, people who were unemployed, people with mental illnesses, and families with badly behaved kids—were excluded from this housing.

In the 1950s, things started to change. Big apartment buildings, set apart from everything else in the city, started popping up.

Jane's neighborhood in Greenwich Village and her childhood Main Street in Dunmore were very different, but both shared something in common: they were places that met the functional needs of the people who lived there. Buildings with a lot of different uses were mixed up together in one community. There were apartments, shops, businesses, and restaurants, all within reach.

After the Federal Housing Act passed in 1934, lenders began to consider this kind of built environment (also known as mixed-use zoning) to be less and less desirable. They stopped funding it. Instead, they funded places that had separated out all of the uses of a city (also known as single-use zoning). At best, people in power were trying (in a misguided way) to solve issues of overcrowding, disease, noise, and pollution. At worst, they were systematically segregating communities in order to drive out people labeled as undesirable.

For people who secured a spot in one of these new kinds of buildings, it was harder to get around—to get from a towering apartment complex to a corner store. It was now illegal to operate a business out of your home. The distance to schools, work, and transportation became even greater. Everyday life became harder.

The government made new rules about who could live in public housing: the middle class was no longer welcome. Public housing became something for low-income people, and increasingly, it was being built to house Black people, immigrants, and people of color. These new developments were not only segregated but also less cared for. They were built closer to industrial areas and toxic pollutants.

Roadway expansion, racist housing policies, and single-use zoning led to a drastic change in the way our communities were built and who could benefit from these building projects.

And it was all perfectly legal.

* * *

The urban renewal program was the government's way of tearing old buildings down to build "anew." It was a top-down approach to city development and destruction that was popularized in the middle of the twentieth century. By 1967, over one million homes had been demolished thanks to urban renewal. These were dwellings that were cleared to make way for highways and public housing.

After World War II, when wealthier people moved out of the city for the rapidly expanding suburbs, many people were left behind, living in poor, overcrowded conditions. The Housing Act of 1949 was meant to fix the lack of growth and opportunity in urban communities. It was a promise, too, to house every American family who needed a home. But this was a case of a cure being worse than the disease.

Here's how it worked. A politician or government official might be uneasy about a city neighborhood, a place they'd call "blight" or a "slum." They'd get the legal permission to knock down the buildings, clear out the area, and make the necessary room to build something brand new. Neighborhoods were often redeveloped to create high-density, high-rise housing separated from the street grid. People lost their homes—*but the new houses and businesses would make up for it!* At least, that was their hope. And there was a lot of money available.

People believed in urban renewal as the way of the future, including Jane's bosses at the magazine. Among their heroes was a man named Ed Logue, an urban planner and city official who made over big sections of American cities. He was an urban renewal guy.

In Boston, Logue masterminded the Government Center, an eyesore that would house City Hall. Logue was banking on the idea that no one would miss what used to be there before. The only cost of this new development? The entire neighborhood of Scollay Square—an area he figured would show the least resistance to developers' so-called improvements.

In New Haven, Logue displaced people to build a suburban shopping center right in the heart of downtown. This was a mall for people in cars, who would pop off the highway and park in the garage. To a person walking on the street, it was an uninviting box.

Jane remembered a meeting with Logue in New Haven. "The best thing that could happen to San Francisco would be another earthquake and a fire," she remembers him telling her.

Meaning he thought the entire city should be wiped out. To Jane, Logue was a fool. And a cruel one, at that. But it took her years to really understand this.

* * *

Jane was a bit of a cheerleader for urban renewal early on. She wrote about these projects in a positive light.

So what changed for Jane? How did she find herself arguing with colleagues, dismayed at the evidence before her in her city laboratory?

In 1956, she connected with a person who changed how she thought about these projects, how she thought about cities, and how she thought about, well, everything. His name was William H. Kirk. He ran a social service agency in East Harlem called Union Settlement.

Jane credits Kirk as being one of the first people to show her how city streets work. They watched the streets and sidewalks together. They watched the kids play stick ball and the women pin laundry to the fire escape of the walk-up row houses. They watched the comings and goings from the salon, candy shops, social clubs, and meat markets. They watched people.

So why Kirk? And why now?

In the 1950s, Black, Puerto Rican, and white families (mostly Italian immigrants) were living together in cramped quarters in East Harlem. Homes there lacked basic amenities like heat, and crime was rampant. During this period in city-building, New York was doubling down on large-scale, towering housing projects. The people in charge were bent on transforming East Harlem, the epicenter of urban renewal in the country at the time. The racist narrative they were spewing and believing—and worse, getting other people to believe? *We'll save these people from themselves!*

But Kirk wasn't buying it. Yes, there were lots of problems in East Harlem. But the solution was worse.

Years later, Kirk, Jane, and a few other activists developed mixed-use housing projects that were nothing like the big towers in the middle of an empty unused park space. He wanted to prove that there was another way to add city housing that was affordable as well as a place where people would want to live. The proposal was promptly dismissed, but Jane was very inspired by his ideas for new housing. People of different races and incomes were living together, and their homes were integrated into the cityscape alongside shops and businesses. This was "inclusive" and "equitable" housing before the terms were widely used, as they are today.

"By showing me East Harlem, [Kirk] showed me a way of seeing other neighborhoods, and downtowns too," Jane said in the introduction of her famous book, describing him as an influential force on her understanding of the "order" of cities. Her use of the word "order" is interesting. She's using it to represent what looked like chaos to others—a lively, bustling city street, filled with people coming and going, hanging out, and participating alongside one another in their shared community.

To Jane, order was organized complexity.

And she had William Kirk as a guide to help her see this.

* * *

Urban renewal was problematic in many ways. But central to its failure was someone at the top telling ordinary people how they should live.

It was a dream of the way something ought to be, untethered from the reality of the way things are. "You can't create the texture of a living city in one fell swoop that way. Things must grow," Jane later wrote. "All plans—business, your children's education, whatever—are made like this, playing it by ear along the way." Urban renewal lacked the improvisation that real planning requires. Its disciples were obsessed with the idea of perfection.

Because of the racist (and legal) practices of redlining, the neighborhoods that Black people and immigrants were moving into (and white people were fleeing) were quickly becoming run-down and under-resourced. Government disinvestment caused businesses to shutter. The FHA gave out home improvement loans only to white people.

It was a vicious cycle caused by policies that planners and politicians exploited for money and power. And the very people who lost the most from government disinvestment faced another challenge: they could be kicked out of their home entirely.

"Urban renewal means Negro removal," the poet, writer, and voice of the Civil Rights movement James Baldwin said in a 1963 interview. While the federal government funded massive, single-use housing projects, they simultaneously used their power to tear down Black and immigrant communities because . . . they could. (This is called "eminent domain," but we might as well call it Racist Bullying 101.)

And what was left after entire communities were forced out? A future marketed as "progress."

Jane's understanding of urban renewal deepened as she toured new building projects. She visited a construction site of Park West Village on the Upper West Side, pretending to be on the hunt for an apartment. Oh, the promise was clear, all right. Chain-linked fences would provide white middle class people with their very own gated community within the city. She remembered how the agent described the segregated lifestyle as a feature: "All that will go," the realtor said, waving away the existing neighborhood with a hand. "Those people will go. We are the pioneers here."

It was evidence in her arsenal. The meaning of urban renewal was becoming crystal clear.

All of the people that were *for* urban renewal—the city officials, the architects, the developers, the builders, the real estate agents—were people who bought the racist story that the city was "bad."

* * *

One of the places where Jane observed the effects of urban renewal firsthand was in Philadelphia. Each city seemed to have its own urban renewal guy. We'll give Boston and New Haven to Logue. In Philadelphia, Edmund Bacon was the face of so-called progress. His urban renewal projects— projects that were well received at the time—were a source of Jane's growing suspicion.

Like Logue, Bacon's schemes had some merit, and Jane first wrote about these small urban renewal projects approvingly.

But something wasn't sitting right.

Jane observed the deserted streets surrounding these new towering projects. She witnessed the desolation. She could hear William Kirk—all that he had taught her loomed large as she took the emptiness in.

Write, revise, rework.

All of the evidence was pointing to something else.

Revise.

Rewrite.

What's really *happening here?* she asked.

Jane noticed that neighboring streets—older streets with shorter blocks that were part of the city grid—were lively and filled with people.

On tour in Philadelphia with Bacon, she was dismayed to see a boy, all alone, kicking a tire in the open green space below a huge, towering apartment complex. No one else was in sight. Alarmed at the empty scene before her, she wondered, *Where are all the people?*

Jane used the pages of *Architectural Forum* to ask the questions that burned hot for her: What good could come from a place where the neighborhood had been erased?

She asked the planners: *Why will you tear down neighborhoods brimming with activity, and build new housing projects that feel like ghost towns?*

Why didn't they see what she saw?

* * *

In the late 1950s, Jane returned to the North End of Boston. It had been a good twenty years since she had last visited, and she couldn't believe her eyes.

Her interest in, and admiration of, this particular neighborhood (home to immigrants from Ireland, Eastern Europe, and, later, Sicily) is well documented throughout many chapters of her book *Death and Life*.

On her first visit, Jane found the neighborhood filled with "badly overcrowded" tenements with mattresses pushed against the windows. The people were "desperately poor."

But something had happened in the two decades that had passed. Flats were less crowded with people. Fresh paint adorned the walls both inside and out, even in the spaces near parking lots between buildings. Many of the apartments were renovated with updated kitchens and bathrooms.

The neighborhood itself bordered the bustling industry of Boston's waterfront, and the streets—they were alive. Mixed together with apartments were shops, services, and markets, Jane recalled. "The general street atmosphere of buoyancy, friendliness, and good health was so infectious," she said.

What was vibrant to Jane was a disgrace to the planning professionals. To them, the North End was "officially considered Boston's worst slum and civic shame," Jane wrote. She went on, with great sarcasm: "It embodies attributes which all enlightened people know are evil because so many wise men have said they are evil."

The planners were a looming threat to North Enders. They saw homes in the neighboring community of West End get ripped to shreds and knew they were next.

And for what? North End was a community with the greatest number of dwellings in all of Boston. There were old buildings. People lived above shops. The children played in the streets, short blocks that latticed the neighborhood.

Jane was so taken by the place and the people she met on her visit there that she used the telephone in a local bar to call a Boston planner.

"Who funded all of these renovations and upgrades?" she asked. "What bank is giving out loans here?"

"Why in the world are you down in North End?" he asked her. He went on. No one would fund that slum. Well . . . there *was* money earmarked for the North End. Bulldozing money, he shared.

Urban renewal was an Emperor Has No Clothes type of scam. It was the kind of charade that had politicians, bankers, architects, academics, and city planners thinking, *Well, those people who are more knowledgeable say so, so it must be so.*

While residents fixed up their homes with their own pennies, the powers that be were trying desperately to paint a different picture. Down below in the cellar storage of a townhouse, beneath the homes of people who were about to lose them, Jane watched as the engineers staged photos.

Pile that junk here, one of them said.

Pull in the trash and debris from the street and frame the shot so this looks like a real dump, said the other.

Jane watched as they skipped right on by the homes of the people who had just applied a fresh coat of paint.

She saw the looks in the faces of the residents too. It was a mix of fear and anger—but mostly it was a look of people who wanted nothing to do with the men coming in with their cameras and notepads.

The reality of life in the North End was far different from what planners said it was. "The streets of the North End of Boston . . . are probably as safe as any place on earth in this respect," Frank Havey, the director of a local settlement house, told Jane.

Even the city planner Jane spoke to couldn't account for the neighborhood's puzzling successes.

Yes, it was the most affordable neighborhood in Boston, he admitted.

Yes, it had a death rate lower than the city average.

But it was still a slum, he emphasized.

"You should have more slums like this," Jane said.

The weird thing was that the planner agreed with her— to a point. He told her how he like to hang out in the North End, to get a feel for the "cheerful street life."

You might think he'd find value and worth in a place he visited for fun.

But no.

He insisted on tearing down the streets and the houses there, and starting all over instead.

* * *

As a woman reporting in a male-dominated field, Jane faced her fair share of misogyny, enough to last a lifetime. The backlash from the male planners was ironic. Overly emotional reactions on their part? Check. Hysteria? Check. Naïveté? Yes, that too. These responses to her work and ideas were blows that came with the territory as she spoke her mind.

It was the men, in fact, who were unable to evolve in the face of real evidence. Jane could remove herself from what she observed: it wasn't personal to her. But she watched as the men who placed a bad bet clung on to their original ideas. They were simply unable to shift their thinking. This new way of looking at urban renewal was, according to Jane, "a terrible threat to them. I don't think it's so much of an intellectual threat, but an emotional threat: their whole worldview will have to go through that upsetting thing of being confused."

It was easier to overlook anything and anyone who contradicted them.

It was much easier to overlook Jane than to face the truth.

* * *

Big housing projects began sprouting up throughout New York City and across the nation. A whole new world was emerging.

"As an extreme example, New York housing agencies have spent something close to $250 million on rebuilding in East Harlem, without spending anything to find out what they were really up to—neither what they were really destroying, nor what they were really creating," Jane wrote.

Urban renewal projects in New York, Boston, Philadelphia, and St. Louis were being marketed to the public as neighborhood improvements, ones that posed just a slight disruption to the residents who were forced to move. Developers worked quickly to push these projects through city hall. They cleared out the old to make way for the new: towering apartment buildings, surrounded by unused, open space. People were losing their homes and entire neighborhoods were being destroyed.

Decades later, by the time of Jane's death in 2006, it was common knowledge that the ideas behind urban renewal were misguided and unfounded. (In Jane's obituary, the *New York Times* compared it to the outdated, harmful practice of bloodletting.) But in the 1950s, those who were against urban renewal were falsely characterized as people against progress.

Jane saw for herself what these projects were doing to the lives of people facing eviction. In 1958, Jane was sent to the West End of Boston to cover a new housing project that would replace the buildings already existing there. (The new buildings would be much taller and were meant to house people with low and moderate incomes.)

But the working-class people who lived in Boston's West End didn't want to lose their homes. They wanted to stay in their community. *How could* this *be considered progress?* Jane thought.

When Jane spoke with the architects about what was really happening, even *they* couldn't convince themselves that what they were doing was the right thing. One of them told Jane that it was heartbreaking that such beautiful, old buildings would be replaced by something inferior. (Never mind the disruption to the newly unhoused.)

Another revealed the deception that was involved in making a case for slum clearance. "I had to get down on my hands and knees in the crawl spaces so I could get photos that looked dark and dreary," he told her, describing how entire neighborhoods were portrayed as horrendous, infested health hazards. To Jane, it was complete and utter dishonesty in the service of some misguided faith in urban renewal.

A price needed to be paid sometimes to achieve greatness, the architects argued.

"Why is urban renewal a greater good?" she asked them.

It was as if she was asking why the sky was blue. Because "slums are bad," they told her.

"But this isn't a slum," Jane insisted. They had *just* told her how they were staging photos to make it look like one.

"Oh well," they said, leaving it at that.

Jane was angry. She was angry because the architects were lying, and she was angry because they lacked any curiosity about real life.

But anger can be a good thing. It can show you what you care about, and what's worth fighting for.

* * *

The city planners looked at urban renewal as a sacrifice that was necessary on a community's journey toward the common good.

But Jane saw through this: the planners couldn't tell her how they defined the common good. And how could they even call it that, if the people being displaced wouldn't be the ones to reap the benefits from some idealized city?

When Jane asked a city planner about the families who would be kicked out, he told her, "You can't make an omelet without breaking eggs."

Jane was furious. *These are people, not eggs*, she said. *And if we're supposed to be helping people by improving their homes, then they should be better off, not worse off, in the end.*

She was making connections and weighing the evidence. *This urban renewal thing is gutting us*, she thought. *We're decimating our cities.*

She found no allies, but it was not for lack of trying. *Let's not jump to conclusions about how things are supposed to work—let's watch how the world actually works*, she told her colleagues.

Housing development in East Harlem. A similar photo of East Harlem housing was included in Jane's article in Architectural Forum (a version of her Harvard speech) in June, 1956. THE MUNICIPAL ARCHIVES, CITY OF NEW YORK

"I got quite a lot of alibis," she later said of this time. She couldn't convince them.

The planners were very much still disciples of this new vision for the city.

"There was almost no inquiry being made into the sense, if any, behind the orthodox theories of planning, housing, and urban design," she said in 1961. "There seemed to be almost no curiosity, except on the most superficial level, about how big cities work."

Urban renewal was a vision that must have given some

planners a sense of purpose in their life, she later said. "They wanted to live in an exciting new world."

But it never should have been about the planners, or the developers, or the federal government. All of these people believed they knew best, but they were not the experts of a city that wasn't theirs in the first place.

Jane Jacobs keenly observed a decade of city "rebuilding," and the jury was in. In July 1955, before she was well-known, before she had the ear of the world, before she had even met William Kirk in East Harlem, she wrote in the pages of *Architectural Forum*: "Hundreds of thousands of people with hundreds of thousands of plans and purposes built the city and only they will rebuild the city."

CHAPTER 5

AND THE CROWD GOES WILD

"I was talking on television with a planner from upstate
New York not long ago who was saying how grand and
vital urban renewal is. And I said to him, 'Name me
one urban renewal project that is really successful.' He
thought for a while and finally named a project that
doesn't exist yet. It's just a plan. And I said, 'No, the plans
are always full of people doing just what you want, that's
the thing about plans. Name me a project that's been
built. A lot have been built by now.' And he couldn't."

—JANE JACOBS[1]

Jane told herself that she would never do it: she would never—
ever—give a speech. Writing down her ideas and seeing them
out there, in the world, in print? Well, that was different. You
weren't eye to eye with your readers, seeing them staring at
you. You weren't faced with a room full of men with fancy
degrees who thought that they were better than everyone else.

But life doesn't always line up with your comfort zone.
Sometimes the very thing you should do is also the thing
that's really difficult to do.

Jane's boss, Douglas Haskell, was scheduled to give a talk at an urban design conference at Harvard. But something came up. He had to leave town, so he asked her to fill in.

That's the other thing about life: sometimes something as mundane as a schedule conflict can be *the* moment that changes everything.

To be clear, it wasn't just luck that launched Jane into the spotlight. Haskell could have picked any colleague, but he chose Jane. She was the one out of all of them who knew the most about urban renewal.

She was the one who had done her homework *and* the extra credit.

* * *

Jane *hated* speaking in public. She had terrible stage fright.

I don't want to do this, she told Haskell.

But work was work, and her managing editor told her that she had to go.

So she relented.

With one (important) condition.

I can do exactly what I want with my ten minutes.

* * *

When it came time to walk up to the podium, Jane felt nervous. The room was full of powerful architects, designers, writers, and thinkers.

These were men who believed in their theories and ideas like a religion. "The great men of planning and its philosophy—Ebenezer Howard, Le Corbusier, Lewis Mumford, and the others—deplored cities, were disgusted by their streets, and even sought to erase them as far as possible," Jane wrote later in life.

These were men who *hated* the city.

And one of them—Lewis Mumford himself—was staring right at her from his seat in the audience.

The whole thing lasted ten minutes. It was both a "real ordeal" and a blur. Jane felt like she entered a state of hypnosis.

Urban renewal isn't working, she told her audience. *The experts have it wrong. Architectural plans that are responsible for uprooting fifty thousand people and closing one thousand stores in Harlem alone are harmful, not beautiful.*

What happens when we make our cities like the suburbs? she asked them. *When we wipe out the city block—and the markets, the delis, the fruit stands, and shops—for an isolated apartment tower over here, and a supermarket someplace else?*

Lost are the thirty shopkeepers who perform an essential public function on streets and sidewalks beyond their front door.

Lost is the communal space where children gather to buy lollipops and adults connect over a coffee or beer.

Lost are "the hand-to-mouth cooperative nursery schools, the ballet classes, the do-it-yourself work-shops, the little exotic stores which are among the great charms of a city," she said.

She went on: *Our neighborhoods shouldn't be wiped out in favor of a grand design that is more like a suburban superblock, erasing the history, vibrancy, and life from a community.*

In East Harlem, she told them, *two thousand people in a housing project have one single communal space in which to gather: the laundry room in the basement. This is design at its most appalling, creating "social poverty beyond anything the slums ever knew,"* she said.

Jane's speech wasn't just a firestorm of complaining and finger-pointing. She went on to give real, concrete suggestions, rooted in the history of how humans have lived and gathered and traded for thousands of years. *Think about the stoops and the sidewalks and the shopfronts that you are ripping up,* she told them. *Think about the Roman plaza, marketplace, and the forum. Think about the intimacy in public space that is on the cutting room floor in the name of progress.*

Mailboxes, laundry rooms, and playgrounds? These aren't "seemingly trivial conveniences" for you to hide. Show them off. Show them how life really works, she says.

And what about the long stretch of park space surrounding tall apartment "towers"? A total bore. Make it as vital as the streetscape, or it's just not good enough.

This whole idea of bringing the suburb into the city? Well—"This is a ludicrous situation," she told them. "And it ought to give planners the shivers."

Jane publicly disagreed with the popular, accepted ideas of the day—to the very people who were actively promoting these ideas. She showed them a glimpse of what a rebuilt city could really look like.

The room was silent, each word a puncture to the status quo.

The way things are.

The way we do things.

But the silence broke, and became a roar.

The crowd erupted in . . . *applause.*

"It was a big hit because nobody had heard anybody saying these things before, apparently," she said about her watershed speech in an interview toward the end of her life. "I had hypnotized myself, but I had apparently hypnotized them too." She didn't just get through it—she stuck the landing. "I believed what I was saying."

It was a daring move, and it worked.

With this one speech, Jane got people talking—about old ideas that were new again.

And it really got the architects and planners and developers talking about *her.*

* * *

The Harvard speech turned a page in the story of Jane's life.

Along with the applause and acclaim, there were those who completely misunderstood her point. Some city planners clutched to her ideas, interpreting them as unspoken support for whatever they were planning to do in the first place. In the book *Vital Little Plans*, a collection of Jane's writings, editors Samuel Zipp and Nathan Storring tell the story of the proud planners who revised their design for a segregated, isolated high-rise housing complex by plopping in one lone corner store to their drawing.

See, we did what you said! they seemed to say to Jane with their new, updated plan.

But adding a feature here or removing an element there wouldn't cut it.

Jane was asking the city planners to rethink their entire belief system.

* * *

I keep hearing about this woman, William H. Whyte, an editor at *Fortune* magazine, told his colleagues. His fellow writers and editors weren't convinced that Jane Jacobs was really worth paying much attention to. But Whyte wouldn't let it go. *Who is she? What else does she have to say?*

Whyte invited her to the offices of *Fortune* for a meeting. She didn't have a ton of experience, but her ideas impressed him. *She's never really written anything very long,* Whyte explained to his colleagues. But Whyte wanted her voice in his magazine. He pushed for her, convincing the assigning editors to take a chance on her. Whyte was passionate about cities and wanted to understand how they work. Jane was a new voice with something original to say.

And he felt that the world needed to hear it.

* * *

It must have felt good for Jane to write, to tell the truth, to say it how it was. Years of reporting in East Harlem and in Philadelphia had brought her to this point in her career. *Finally,* she was able to formulate her ideas about cities based on facts and the lived experiences of city residents.

Central to her argument was the idea that successful cities, when you take the time to truly look at them, are made up of lots of small, working, livable communities.

"You've got to get out and walk," she wrote. "Walk, and you will see that many of the assumptions on which the projects depend are visibly wrong."

Jane was talking about the dreams of an elite few for a city reimagined—for them, it was a dirty city that needed to be fixed and rebuilt. A messy city cleaned up with a huge, sweeping park. The sloppy-looking mishmash of butchers, repair shops, and convenience stores wiped away for something more orderly. "They will have all the attributes of a well-kept, dignified cemetery," she wrote (in case you weren't clear as to exactly how awful these plans were to her).

Jane covered a lot of ground in her article for *Fortune*, and even praised a handful of not-so-small projects. She riffed on Rockefeller Center ("it respects the street") and wrote admiringly of an "enlivening" plan in Fort Worth, Texas, by the architect Gruen ("it has old buildings mixed with new").

The recipe is simple, she stated, over and over again: "The best way to plan for downtown is to see how people use it today; to look for its strengths and to exploit and reinforce them," she wrote. Only at street level, down here, can we "see what people like."

And it's those very same people who should decide—must decide—what their vision of their dream city will be. "Rarely before has the citizen had such a chance to reshape the city," she wrote, "and to make it the kind of city that he likes and that others will too."

Jane devoted only a few brief paragraphs of the *Fortune* article to Lincoln Center, the Metropolitan Opera's new home slated to wipe out a superblock—then home to thousands of people, many of them Black and Puerto Rican—on the Upper West Side.

It's not as if Jane was against cultural institutions or entertainment venues like libraries, museums, sporting arenas, or concert halls. She was very much *for* integrating these kinds of essential neighborhood outposts into the community as opposed to isolating them from the city street. But she was against the displacement that this project would inevitably cause.

Jane's jab against Lincoln Center was a small part of the article, and she didn't even mention the culprit behind the project by name.

However few words she had to say about the project that would eventually evict seven thousand people and shutter eight hundred businesses, her criticism was a bold move. Jane used her platform writing for a mainstream national magazine to begin openly criticizing one of the most influential city planners in New York City at the time.

The man behind the supersized project was Robert Moses.

* * *

Described as the most powerful man in New York who never held office, Robert Moses spearheaded projects that impacted almost every part of a New Yorker's life—and still do to this day. He built housing projects, highways, bridges, tunnels, state parks, beaches, playgrounds, and pools throughout the city and beyond. Included in this long list of architectural accomplishments are Jones Beach, Riverside Park, the Triborough Bridge, the Harlem River Drive, West Side Highway, the Long Island Expressway, the Cross Bronx Expressway, the Throgs Neck Bridge, the

Henry Hudson Bridge, the Verrazzano-Narrows Bridge, Lincoln Center, the United Nations Plaza, Shea Stadium, the New York Coliseum, and Central Park's Conservatory Garden, Great Lawn, and Zoo.

Whew.

Robert Moses's legacy and impact on city planning was arguably as great as Jane's. And it would be almost impossible to tell Jane Jacobs's story without telling the story of her lifelong rival and opponent.

* * *

As a kid, if Jane needed to get somewhere, she'd get herself there. Meaning, she'd take her bike, walk, or hop on the streetcar. Not much had changed for adult Jane, who took the New York City subway or biked to get around.

From her home in the Village, Jane rode her bicycle through the Flower District, Garment District, and cluster of department stores to *Forum*'s Midtown offices. This was all before protected bike lanes; the biographer Robert Kanigel described her preference to ride to work as completely "outlandish." "Watch out girlie, you'll get hurt!" or "Get a horse!" were just some of the unwelcome comments Jane was used to hearing as she rode uptown.[2]

And it's likely she thought *a lot* about Moses and his plans for New York on her bicycle rides uptown to the *Forum* offices.

Jane on her bicycle, Washington Street, 1963. BOB GOMEL/GETTY

But Moses? No. He would have never taken a bicycle to work. He didn't even take the subway. Moses relied on a very different way of getting around: his chauffeur would take him by car, just as he had since he was a boy. And he probably didn't spend a single moment thinking about Jane Jacobs on his morning ride to the office.

Robert Moses was born in New Haven, Connecticut, and moved with his family to New York City in 1897 when he was nine years old. He came from a well-off household that employed servants and cooks in their five-story brownstone in Midtown Manhattan. Having a driver was a necessity he likely never questioned—to Moses, the automobile was *the* way to get where you wanted to go. (Which is ironic, because he never learned how to drive a car himself.)

Driving was at the center of Moses's belief system and was baked into every idea and architectural project he took on.

To Moses, New York City needed serious help.

And the only way to fix it was to reshape it around his favorite toy.

The cure for the city was the car, of course.

* * *

While young Jane Butzner scrambled to find work in New York City, pounding the pavement with her stenography certificate in hand, young Robert Moses took a very different path up the stepladder of his career, which culminated in his role as New York City's master developer.

Both Moses and Jane were charming, whip-smart intelligent, and demonstrated literary aspirations early in life. But, unlike Jane, Moses was a stand-out student.

An all-around young adult and promising athlete at prep school, Moses went on to study at Yale as an undergrad. Later, he attended the prestigious Oxford University and earned a PhD in political science from Columbia (about twenty-five years before Jane was told she could no longer pursue a degree there because of her poor high school grades).

Like Jane, Moses held a variety of different positions during his early years of working in New York City. But Moses had the freedom to take on unpaid volunteer work in order to gain invaluable experience and establish professional connections. He also had the freedom to risk losing his job. Case in point: at a job he held during World War I, Moses couldn't make sense of how or why his boss was running things. So he spoke up, telling his employer that the company's systems were inefficient—an act of insubordination that got him fired.

What would have been devastating to another was no big deal for Moses. He had no problem keeping himself, his wife, and his growing family of children afloat.

That was what his family's money was for.

* * *

In the 1950s, America was not living up to its promise of "equality for all." Not everyone was considered deserving of equal rights, or able to safely voice their opposition against an outside force telling them how they should live. The city was indeed on the cusp of a new era of major housing projects in 1958. Poverty swept through the city as "white flight" took hold.

In New York City, developers like Moses and the city officials who rubber-stamped their schemes were outright gutting the existing neighborhoods and ruining the lives of people who lived there.

"I'd tear 'em all out, every bit of 'em," Moses said about his plans for Harlem. "I say that you have a cancerous growth there that has to be carved out."

This idea of an "inner city"—a racist term used to incorrectly cast Black neighborhoods as unsafe and dirty—was an image that Moses used to his advantage. It was all part of his strategy to reshape New York by making way for new public parks and infrastructure like highways and bridges.

Like a wizard waving a magic wand, he'd mark certain neighborhoods as uninhabitable, regardless of how the people who lived there felt. The condemned neighborhoods would be stuck in a limbo of sorts until the bulldozers arrived—businesses wouldn't dare consider investing, the economy would worsen, and finally residents would be forced to move.

There was just no way around it, no way of avoiding it, Moses unapologetically told the few skeptics. He even pulled out the old-people-are-eggs metaphor that at least one other planner had used: "I hail the chef who can make omelets without breaking eggs."

That wasn't Moses's only mean-spirited (and, frankly, weird) food reference. To build a new city when an existing city is in its way, he said, "you have to hack your way with a meat ax."

Destruction was the cure.

And people were the sacrifice.

* * *

So how was Robert Moses able to accomplish all of this?

Remember: he never held office. He was never elected by the people of New York.

Yet Moses wielded tremendous political power in New York from the 1920s through the 1960s. He did this by relying on his network of friends in high places. His buddies appointed him to positions that gave him oversight over demolition *and* rebuilding. No one could keep him in check because he ran the whole show.

Homes, roads, bridges, tunnels—it was all the same approach. Complete control. He ran the Triborough Bridge and Tunnel Authority, a corporation that funds, builds, and operates bridges and tunnels in New York City. Robert Moses oversaw the toll collection of the seven bridges throughout the city and funneled money right back into a special bridge and tunnel police force. By having his thumb on something as significant as car entry into Manhattan, he could do whatever he pleased with the money he was raking in. And it wasn't going to more train tracks, that's for sure. If you wanted a definition of conflict of interest, Robert Moses was a living and breathing example.

In *Death and Life*, Jane wrote about his "genius at getting things done." While she couldn't have been more aghast at some of his "accomplishments," she acknowledged that Moses was the master of the power play. He controlled public money while schmoozing with elected officials to get them to bend to his will.

But it wouldn't be totally fair to put all of the blame on Moses: the elected officials were just as culpable.

Many actively disregarded the best interests of the people they were supposed to serve.

They were bought and sold.

* * *

Master developer, accomplished builder, shaper of New York, slum-clearance czar, car fanatic, builder of great parks, political powerhouse. These are just some of the ways that we can look at Moses.

Moses used his power and privilege to target communities with less political power. His grand plan for New York included the demolition of neighborhoods of Black people, people of color, and immigrants—many of the same people who were shut out of American homeownership through the racist practices of redlining and mortgage discrimination.

Half a million people were displaced under his urban renewal projects and about a quarter of a million more lost their homes for the highway projects that cut through the city. Over and over, Moses deliberately blocked transit and subway projects in favor of a city and region that, in his mind, should only be accessible by car.

Displacement was devastating for people who were in Robert Moses's way. But their troubles didn't end there. Moses also built new public housing away from the city center. Cloaked as a so-called opportunity for low-income families, this housing only systematically segregated New York further.

What's the problem? Moses wondered out loud. "A fellow who gets up in the upper stories of a public housing project where he has a view, what's the matter with him?" Moses told a reporter. "He's got a nice place to live, hasn't he?"

* * *

But let's not stop there. (Yes, there's more.) Moses built pools for "the public" with federal money and tried to keep Black people out of them. In East Harlem, he ordered the custodians of the Thomas Jefferson Pool to keep the water temperature low, based on his racist belief that African American people did not like cool water.

Robert Caro, author of *The Power Broker*, the extensively researched portrait of Robert Moses published in 1974, called Moses "the most racist human being I had ever really encountered."

Once, while Caro waited for Moses to finish a telephone call, he watched as Moses slammed the receiver down while turning to Caro to say: "They expect me to build playgrounds for that scum floating up from Puerto Rico."

* * *

We can keep going. He not only did pools, he made beaches too. In theory, Jones Beach—a public beach meant to give ordinary people access to the beautiful natural world of the Atlantic seashore—was a grand idea.

It was Moses's idea, and there was much to be admired about it on the surface.

But Moses made a deliberate decision to make Jones Beach inaccessible. He built miles of seashore shouldered by endless parking lots. He passed on opportunities to connect public transit to the beaches, and built the bridges on the parkways so low that only cars could get to the beach.

Bridge height seems like an unimportant architectural detail. But if you stood on the beach, like Caro did, you would have only seen white people. According to Caro, Moses knew full well what he was doing: buses couldn't fit under the low-slung overpasses, so only people who could afford a car made it to the water.

Other historians suggest that the low bridges were a result of Moses's love of the scenic, "cinematic" parkway experience that he felt a motorist should experience on their way to nature—that it wasn't a deliberately racist move. Even Jane excused his obsession with the car as a matter of timing—his own coming of age coincided with the radical transformation of culture and society during the Automobile and Industrial Ages. Just as "some belles, when they are old ladies, still cling to the fashions and coiffures of their exciting youth," Jane wrote, Moses couldn't let go of the car.

But Caro told the *Gothamist* in an interview in 2016 that Moses didn't want poor people of color on the public beach, plain and simple. He remembers Moses's aide telling him that legislation preventing buses on highways can always be rewritten—but once a bridge is up, it's going to be really difficult to get that rebuilt.

* * *

For three decades, Robert Moses amassed enormous power and then systematically wielded it against the citizenry itself. He resisted the idea of the organic evolution and expansion of his city, built over time, for and by ordinary people. In 1981, the writer Gwinn Owens wrote about Moses's legacy in the *Baltimore Sun*: "He really did not understand the delicate spider web of human interaction that makes a city work."

Moses was, during this period especially, adored by influential New Yorkers. Businessmen, politicians, academics, thought leaders, and journalists couldn't get enough of his bold ideas and action.

He was *the* man.

In 1958, when Jane's criticism of his Lincoln Center project hit newsstands, Moses was at the apex of his power. To Moses, Jane Jacobs was laughable, just some mom who was stirring up trouble. She was no threat at all.

But for Jane, Moses's disdain and indifference for ordinary

people was the rotting core that pervaded the city's problems. She saw the gang of white male city planners as lemmings going off the ledge, fawning over their superstar. "Every so often," she wrote in *Architectural Forum* in 1957, "things 'everybody knows' need to be reexamined."

It was time to reexamine.

It was time to turn the lens on the guy who always got his way. To really look at what he was doing and how deeply devastating it was.

It was time for Jane Jacobs to take on Robert Moses, the most powerful man in New York.

CHAPTER 6

MOTHERS VS. MOSES

"Today everyone who values cities is disturbed by
automobiles."

—JANE JACOBS[1]

"When traffic gets worse, the strategy is to provide more
highways, more ways for more automobiles to get into
the city. It's self-defeating. The whole system has its tail
in its mouth. It's guaranteed not to solve the problem but
to add to it."

—JANE JACOBS[2]

Jane's neighbors, Edith Lyons and Shirley Hays, adored
their open space in the heart of Greenwich Village, Washington Square Park. Removed from the hustle and bustle
on the adjacent streets, with a view of the grand archway
built a half century before, the park was their family's place to play and see friends in the 1950s. The park
was—and is—*the* center of the Village. Its magnetism
was owed to its location and the diversity of New Yorkers
who frequented it: artists, NYU students, kids, and really

anyone who needed a moment's rest in a pocket of green parkland.

Fifth Avenue was the main road that, at the time, ran through the park, but Moses had his eye on something *much* bigger. He wanted to build a four-lane highway that tore through the middle of the park. Car speed was the name of the game, and everything had to be sacrificed in this effort.

Maybe Moses still felt the sting of defeat from decades earlier, when he tried (unsuccessfully) to destroy the park by expanding the roads around it into fast-moving expressways.

Locals fought him then and won. Twenty years later, he was at it again, with an even more destructive plan. But Moses had amassed a tremendous amount of power in that time. City officials were now bowing to the idea because of the man behind it.

Like a parent offering "choices" to a toddler, the city asked Edith, Shirley, and their neighbors: *Which alternative do you prefer? More lanes of roadway through the park, or the widening of the road around it?*

We must address this terrible problem of traffic congestion, the city explained. *We either need make the roads wider, or we need build more roads.*

But Edith and Shirley didn't buy it. Neither choice was good for their park or for their neighbors.

"In 1955 and '56, it was unheard of to fight a thing like the roadway through Washington Square, unheard of to talk in the kind of terms that educated people now find it perfectly natural to talk in," Jane later said about the pair of unconventional, daring women at the helm of the neighborhood effort. Which is to say that Edith and Shirley weren't applauded for their effort. Quite the opposite, actually. When they first spoke out about the park, they were considered crazy and ignorant. Jane remembered how they were dismissed by experts and professionals who thought, *Isn't this just like a woman to think that way?*

They could block his plan again, like their neighborhood did decades earlier. But Edith and Shirley weren't really interested in what had been done before.

Sometimes opposition is not enough. It's too passive, too reactive. Not "pro" anything.

Edith and Shirley's wheels were spinning.

They didn't just want to block something.

They wanted to use this opportunity to activate their community to make their park even better.

* * *

The highway was going to be called Fifth Avenue South and would, according to Moses, bring only good things. Cars would be able to get downtown faster! The economy would improve! Landlords would rake it in with skyrocketing rents! (Ha.)

The logic was absurd, really. Jane knew that his plans would create the opposite effect and choke the neighboring businesses. When a place is built around cars—not people—the people go away. They go somewhere else. "In the traffic for Washington Square, we see how neatly a cancer can be planted," Jane wrote in the *Village Voice* in 1957 about the city's misguided plan.

This wasn't any old park either. The "vital organ" was a magnetic center and a gathering spot for neighborhood kids, the Beat Generation, and Bob Dylan at the start of his musical career.

"I have heard with alarm and almost with disbelief, the plans to run a sunken highway through the center of Washington Square," Jane wrote to Mayor Robert F. Wagner Jr. and the Manhattan borough president in 1955.

"My husband and I are amongst the citizens who truly believe in New York to the extent that we have bought a home in the heart of the city and remodeled it with a lot of hard work. It is very discouraging to do our best to make the city more habitable and then to learn that the city itself is thinking up schemes to make it uninhabitable."

Jane is sometimes portrayed as the leader of the effort, but she wasn't, by any means. When she joined the Committee to Save Washington Square Park (later called the Joint Emergency Committee to Close Washington Square Park to Traffic), it was already well established. Nonetheless, it was a move that would mark the beginning of Jane's ongoing, public battles with Robert Moses.

A People's Guide to Activism (Part I): Save the Square Edition

Almost everyone was against the highway through the park, Jane knew. But this wasn't enough. It wasn't enough to want something different than what the "vandal" (as Jane called Moses) was proposing. "We felt as if we were stuck in flypaper, unable to mobilize effectively the really big support that actually was out there in the community," Jane later said about this moment. Another problem: a few very important people in prominent leadership positions were very much *for* the highway.

How do you organize a broad base of people around an issue? There isn't a one-size-fits-all answer to that question. It's not about a single tactic or a magic pill that fixes everything. Instead, Jane and her neighbors engaged in many approaches implemented together, as a sustained and multipronged effort, over the course of several years. Collectively, they developed on the ground expertise: watching, observing, acting, making mistakes, finding success, and, all the while, improvising.

George Lakey, a writer, professor, and activist who *did* write the actual book on nonviolent direct action, describes campaigns as having three elements: a demand, a target, and escalating tactics.[3] While Jane's generosity with reporters and the work of historians are the primary sources that pin together the following "guide"—especially Jane's interview with Leticia Kent for the Greenwich Village Society for Historic Preservation in 1997—she herself never wrote or compiled such a playbook for organizing. Luckily for us, biography-crafting gives us the permission to do so.

#1. Create a niche committee with a weird name.
Local issues—in this case, a highway running through a park—bring together all kinds of people of various political backgrounds. Republicans and Democrats who would never see eye to eye on national issues might be surprised to find themselves aligned against their local government.

We have a major advantage over them, Jane's fellow organizer, Ray Rubinow, told her. *We can come together on this one issue even though there are a million other issues we might disagree on.* Ray and Jane and others helped shape a committee with a laser focus—a park for people, not cars—as opposed to creating a group that focused on general issues.

How did this tactic help them organize? In the past, Greenwich Village residents who were organizing around an issue would methodically reach out to every local group and committee to get their support. It was a time-consuming process that involved each group reaching consensus (or not) in support of the issue. A lot of time was wasted in this effort with little to show for it, Jane explained.

It was Ray's idea to create the "Joint Emergency Committee to Close Washington Square to All but Emergency Traffic." This may not have been a catchy name, but that wasn't the point. The point was to be specific—so specific that every activist, neighbor, and resident knew exactly what they were putting in their volunteer time for.

"In retrospect, it seems so sensible, so obvious, so natural, and yet it didn't exist before he thought it out, invented it and actually got it working," Jane said of this approach. "After that, it became the model for practically every successful fight we had to wage in Greenwich Village."

#2. Become a neighborhood fixture.
Jane was charged with handing out petitions at local establishments and corner stores. She kept the shopkeepers well-supplied with petition cards, picking up signed cards and replenishing supplies as needed. It was tedious messenger work, but before the era of digital petitions, there wasn't any way around it.

The mood of 1950s McCarthyism was a real obstacle to collecting signatures. *You don't know who else might be signing—it might be dangerous to sign,* Jane remembered a husband telling his wife who stopped at her table in Washington Square. But since the battle for the square persisted over many years, the political atmosphere changed. When the collective fear of McCarthyism dissipated, more people were willing to publicly add their name to a cause.

Today we call this kind of outreach "canvassing" or "grassroots organizing." It's just another way of saying that you show up. You meet people where they are. You explain the issues. You get the message out. Over time, Jane became a trusted public figure of sorts that neighbors would stop on the street to ask for advice on local issues.

Neighborhood fixtures like Jane, Edith, and Shirley are indispensable assets to a hyperlocal cause. They foster important connections that support community needs.

How can we get the city to remove an old, boarded up portable restroom? Mr. Fox, a shop owner, asked Jane while bagging her purchase. Soon Jane found herself in this new position as a community expert.

#3. Use elections.

Community organizing works really well when neighbors get behind a single issue. But when election season came around, those same neighbors who saw eye to eye found themselves bitterly opposed to each other's preferred candidate on the ballot. While voting in public elections is necessary in a democracy, it can create enormous division between friends and neighbors—potential allies.

However, instead of letting local elections dissolve their collective power, the activists battling for Washington Square used the elections to their advantage.

Jane's husband, Bob, was at the very center of this idea. In the middle of the night, sometime during their ongoing battle for the park in the '50s, Bob woke Jane. He couldn't sleep—he was anxious about their game plan. But then it hit him: *We have to make the politicians fearful for their political futures. We have to get them to agree to our terms before the election,* he told her.

Not only did their joint committee not want a highway through the park, they wanted the park *closed* to all traffic except for emergency vehicles. Several politicians were supportive of the idea but none of them really mattered, Bob explained to Jane. The person to focus on was the one who could make this happen. That guy was Bill Passannante, and he was running for reelection for state assemblyman.

The committee's demand couldn't have been clearer: *Stanchions by July 1.** (Stanchions are vertical poles that physically stop traffic from entering a closed off place.) And if Passannante didn't deliver, then what? What kind of leverage did they have? Their leverage was the election. *Do it or we won't reelect you,* they threatened. *You're finished.*

The flip side to this was the praise and accolades Passannante would get if he did deliver. The politician that manages to pull off a positive community change becomes the hero.

#4. Make it temporary.
In order to convince the politician to do the thing you want them to do, it helps if you present the idea as a trial run. Just temporary—nothing the elected official can't undo. But once the thing gets installed—in this case, the stanchions—it will be so universally liked and obvious and

_____

* The actual date—July 1—was just a guess that Jane made later in life in an interview.

well received that they would become unpopular to take the thing away. (Jane credits Bob with this idea too.)

#5. Market your idea.

Empty threats don't really work. Passannante had to *feel* like his reelection could be in jeopardy. What made him believe that Jane and her fellow activists could "ruin" him? They told him simply that they would use "every avenue that we have of public opinion and explaining things" in order to oust him if he wouldn't meet their demand.

The poster said it all: SAVE THE SQUARE! was printed in big bold letters at the top of every sign. A large square in the middle was cut by several lines, representing traffic. In smaller print, the poster read "No Parkway Thru Washington Square Park: CLOSE THE PARK TO ALL TRAFFIC" along with a call to action to send postcards to the mayor and borough president. All of the messaging was clear and to the point. There was no question as to what this fight was all about.

#6. Hold a rally.

A rally is a demonstration of public, collective commitment to and passion for the issue at hand. It is a way of impressing on politicians that there is, in fact, a large body of people behind the neighborhood fixtures they are always hearing from.

Jane and the joint committee decided to hold a rally with this very goal in mind. By design, the rally was intended to make Passannante come around to their idea out of

Save the Square poster documenting the fight to close Washington Square to vehicle traffic in the 1950s. NEW-YORK HISTORICAL SOCIETY

self-protection—not to convince him that it was a good plan for the park. They wanted to make him think, *If I put up a few of these poles, I'll save my job.*

The details that led up to this point (the committee with the superspecific goal, the demands for stanchions by July 1, the threat that politicians would be ousted if they wouldn't comply) would *not* be the focus of the event. All of *that* was happening behind the scenes. The rally was the big public display that was planted at just the right time to demonstrate to the politicians that the joint committee had the entire community behind them.

#7. Center kids.

Kids have been central to protests throughout history. It's a matter of necessity at times, meaning that childcare is not always available to many families who participate in unpaid labor or volunteer work. But often, it's a strategy of organizing in and of itself.

Kids bring enthusiasm and energy to local issues. Their passion is often considered more genuine and less politically motivated. And it happens to be much easier to get signatures when kids ask for them. Children "believed in their cause and it came across," Jane said. "It's hard to resist such sincerity and idealism."

In the battle for Washington Square Park, kids spent many afternoons and weekends on the streets. They plastered billboards and walls with posters advertising the rally. Jane referred to them as her "little elves," and they were very interested in the fight and concerned for the park—a park that was just as much theirs in the first place. Washington Square Park "very much belonged to the children," as Jane said.

#8. Manage your anger . . . or don't.

Go on, Jane! Fight them! the professors at New York University told Jane. *We're behind you!*

Well, they were behind her *in theory*, but wouldn't dare speak out at public hearings—the same meetings at which their employer made statements in favor of *increasing* traffic through the park.

It was surprising, at least at first, for Jane and local organizers to realize that local hospitals and universities were siding with the enemy. But when it came to pushing traffic through the square, these types of institutions fell in line behind the city. They had their eye on a bigger prize: the development of their land to suit their interests. And guess who approves or denies that development? The city, of course. So the administrators of these big players positioned themselves strategically with the city government.

Will you speak? Jane asked these professors who privately backed her.

Well, no . . . they told her. *It wouldn't be wise.*

She tried her best to manage her contempt for these higher education administrators but was less guarded in her writings about the behemoth institutions they worked for. "NYU ought to take a good look at the horrible problems of institutions in some other part of the city, whose neighborhoods have rotted around them," she wrote in the *Village Voice*. To Jane, the NYUs and Columbias were no help, quietly accepting the city's damaging plans to suit their interests.

#9. Make a spectacle.

Passannante took the bait. He decided to close the park to cars on a temporary basis. This was a significant win for the people. But it wasn't the end of the fight.

A couple of newly installed traffic poles aren't exactly

newsworthy, but a few children front and center at a Sunday afternoon ceremony rejoicing for their park that was nearly ruined—now *that* was something to get the reporters and their cameras out.

Instead of a ribbon-cutting ceremony announcing the opening of a new place, the joint committee very cleverly staged a ribbon-*tying* ceremony to honor the closure of the park to cars.

Jane's daughter and joint committee member Norman Redlich's daughter made the symbolic tie in front of four hundred spectators and supporters. Organizer Stanley Tankel drove a vehicle with a sign that read "Last Car Thru Washington Square." The moment was captured by the press, of course, with Manhattan Borough President Hulan E. Jack taking center stage as "the hero" of the day alongside politician Carmine G. DeSapio.

In an almost hilarious, icky politician move, Passannante himself publicly committed "to see that this roadway is never opened again."

#10. Invite the press.

The Jacobs children were front and center at protests, often appearing in photographs of demonstrations in the news just as they had done at the ribbon-tying ceremony.

A few years after the battle for Washington Square, Jane picketed at her daughter's public school, P.S. 41. The school administration, blaming overcrowding issues, had

Jane protesting at P.S. 41, 1964.
FRED W. MCDARRAH/GETTY

decided to transfer fifty-five children who were living in a nearby shelter from P.S. 41 to another school. (The children living in the shelter were awaiting a more permanent living arrangement with their own family or a foster family.) Most of the fifty-five children were Black, while Jane's daughter's school was predominately white.

Jane and other parents organized a protest on the first day of school to bring attention to their demand (allow the children to go back to the school they were previously attending) and proposed solutions (rent space from another building or add an annex to deal with overcrowding).

During the protest, Jane marched into the school building to inform the principal that she would keep her daughter home until the children living in the shelter were permitted to reenroll in their school.

Prior to their public demonstration and demand, Jane and her fellow organizers delivered press releases to newspapers and media, outlining their specific plans.

It may sound unwise, but laying out their plan of action for all to see accomplished two important things. It created doubt and anxiety for the opposing side: *They're doing what?* But it did something that was arguably more impactful: Jane openly spread the word about their plans to protest in order to capture the attention of newspaper reporters and photographers—key players in spreading the word well beyond the walls of the school and PTA meetings.

* * *

But back to the square and the flawlessly executed playbook.

Well, let's be real, there was no playbook. Jane mused on a lot of these ideas much later in life, connecting the dots in hindsight. In the middle, it was murky. It was like taking steps when you can't see what's in front of you.

Remember: all of those city leaders, cheering on the kids like the slippery politicians they were, didn't really think it was a good idea to close the park to cars. They still believed that *increasing* road space would clear up all of the traffic congestion. They went along with this short-term trial run because they wanted to hang on to their political power.

They also thought that the spillover of cars on side streets would create such awful bottlenecks that the neighbors would rise up again, demanding that Moses build the highway after all.

What happened next was a surprise, even to the organizers who were against traffic in the park. The congestion *diminished*. Cars now had to deal with more hassle—the slowness of people crossing and cars parking and deliveries and double parking. By making the area less desirable for drivers, fewer drivers chose to drive through.

If you build something to allow for more cars to pass through—guess what—you get more cars. But the residents and politicians of Greenwich Village watched the opposite play out.

You would think that the city would have woken up to this phenomenon and changed their course, with this experiment unfolding right before them. (Cue laughter.) Unfortunately, there are politicians and transportation engineers *today* who still operate under the rule of thumb that our places need to be designed around moving cars quickly and efficiently, even at a great cost to people and their communities. "Wouldn't it have been interesting if they had looked into this?" Jane said about the politicians who refused to adapt to this new bit of information about how traffic works. But no. They definitely did not look into anything. "The traffic people were completely incurious about what they had done and its effects."

* * *

The effort was an "interminable and horrendous battle," Jane later wrote about the seemingly endless period of her life that she dedicated to saving the park. The iconic photo of the "Last Car Thru" the square was the defining moment of a boots on the ground, yearslong effort against the city.

Moses continued to use every tactic to deflate their efforts, including delaying public hearings. At one of the final public meetings on the matter, about a month or so before the "Last Car Thru," Jane spoke out against traffic through the park at City Hall along with her neighbors Shirley Hayes, Eleanor Roosevelt (former first lady), Margaret Mead (the famous anthropologist), and many others. They delivered thirty thousand signatures from residents against the superhighway through the square, a move that proved impactful. "I'm not opposed to change," Eleanor Roosevelt said on the matter. "In fact, I believe in change. But I think that good tradition has to be preserved."

Moses must have felt that he was losing his grip on what he previously thought was an easy win. It must have infuriated him—expanding a road through a neighborhood with little political power should have been a slam dunk.

He and Jane never met one another. She saw him in

person only once, at a public hearing for the Washington Square Park highway. She remembers the way he held onto the railing, his fist tightening while he shouted. "There's nobody against this," he said as he made one final unsuccessful appeal to the city. "Nobody, nobody, nobody, but a bunch of, a bunch of . . . mothers."

Jane listened as he lashed out at the women who organized against him. But he didn't stay to listen to what *they* had to say. Instead, he left the meeting in disbelief: he never in a million years would have thought that an "inferior group of housewives," as he referred to them, would take him on and win.

* * *

In 1959, four years after Jane signed her first petition to save her beloved park, Robert Moses was forced to scrap his plan entirely. "So pleasant and effective were the results of shutting off Washington Square to traffic that I don't think anybody after that, not that I remember, ever seriously suggested opening the roadway again," Jane said about the temporary measures.

It was almost unbelievable, really.

Jane and her neighbors handed Robert Moses his first real taste of loss. Sure, there had been other setbacks and hurdles before. But this one hurt.

It was a public, stinging loss delivered by the people. The housewives and mothers had won.

CHAPTER 7

A BOOK ABOUT
CITIES

"Cities have the capability of providing something
for everybody, only because, and only when they are
created by everybody."

—JANE JACOBS[1]

The fight for the park was a huge win. But Jane's biggest
accomplishment—arguably the most significant professional accomplishment of her life—still lay ahead.

She was gathering evidence. She was interviewing
experts. The ideas for her seminal work, *The Death and Life
of Great American Cities*, were percolating.

But no great breakthrough occurs in a vacuum. There
were people who came before Jane who criticized urban
renewal. There was William Kirk, the head of Union Settlement in East Harlem, who tried to ring the alarm bells.
He tried to bring attention to the problem: what segregated
public housing *actually* did to people.

And there was Lewis Mumford, the Queens-born philosopher, who had watched Jane's life-changing speech at the urban design conference at Harvard.

Mumford was a well-respected critic, writer, and city planner. And just like Jane, he absolutely loathed what Moses was doing to New York. He regularly spoke out against the towering skyscrapers and massive urban renewal projects in his recurring column in *The New Yorker*, the "Sky Line."

Jane and Mumford were colleagues in a way. They were both writers, with cities as their assigned beat. And early on in their relationship, before Jane was known, he was a mentor to her. Just as Jane began to organize her ideas for *Death and Life*, Mumford wrote Jane a letter telling her that "few people in city planning circles . . . even dimly understand" her "refreshing clarity" and singular point of view. In *The New Yorker*, he applauded her attack of Moses as "devastatingly just" and said that he, too, thought of writing such a public criticism but never got around to it.

Mumford's book, *The Culture of Cities*, was a crash course on the history of cities. He riffed on how to make them better. No one outside of niche urbanist circles really took notice of it when it was published in 1938.

But Jane noticed.

And her observations and writings reflected his own. *How inspiring and exciting to read a fresh voice and expert on cities*, Mumford thought as he read her work. Jane represented the next generation. She was someone who would build upon *his* work and *his* ideas—ideas that predated hers by decades.

Mumford encouraged Jane to go big. "You ought to reach a wider audience for your ideas. Have you thought of the *Saturday Evening Post*?" he wrote in a letter to her in 1958. "There are a half a dozen publishers who would snap up a manuscript of yours on the city," he wrote to her again, just months later.

Jane built on some of Mumford's theses, sure. But she rejected others. If Jane was the future, Mumford was the past.

Perhaps he couldn't see how her work and ideas were diverging from his. Like the city planners he detested, his own biases painted the kind of picture he wanted to see. It was as if Mumford and everyone else was trying to make a big show about what could be done to make the city *less* like a city in the first place.

* * *

Today, people love to tell the story of Jane Jacobs, a mere housewife who wrote a breakout book on the city from her Greenwich Village window, all while she tended to her children. But as Peter Laurence writes in *Becoming Jane Jacobs*, this characterization of her is simply not true. When Jane sat down to write "the book," she was forty-five years old, a professional full-time reporter, and an expert in urban planning and development. It was time to bring her ideas to a wider audience.

"Designing a dream city is easy," Jane wrote as the final line of her breakout *Fortune* magazine article. "Rebuilding a living one takes imagination."

It was a call to action meant to inspire her readers. But someone else took notice in the summer of 1958—a man by the name of Chadbourne Gilpatric, a program officer at the Rockefeller Foundation.

Gil, Jane's nickname for Gilpatric, held this role that was part producer, part agent, part schemer. Best of all, he had deep pockets, thanks to Rockefeller money. He was running an initiative around cities in the 1950s and knew something (or someone) was missing from the chorus of usual voices. Someone like Mumford, but less . . . stodgy. Someone new. Someone who believed in cities as places worth investing in.

Gil was impressed with Jane's article and reached out to her to ask whether there was anything she really wanted to write that she wasn't yet writing. There *was* something, she told him. And that something happened to be *the* book that Jane is best known for today—*The Death and Life of Great American Cities.*

But before it was *the* book, it was a plan for a book. Ideas on paper, not yet executed. Two months after the *Fortune* article hit newsstands, Jane officially proposed an idea to Gilpatric. *The people who are remaking our cities are inspired by their dream suburbs. Not the city itself,* Jane wrote to Gil.

Those first letters to the Rockefeller Foundation are filled with notes on her process. Jane wanted to write a series of ten essays on city streets, based on detailed observations and interviews with individuals on the ground. She'd interview heads of housing developments, former mayors, tenants, and urban thinkers who were more in touch than some of their contemporaries in the clouds. She'd need a year of funding to cover reporting, writing, and editing time.

The Rockefeller Foundation came through, funding Jane and her book on cities. But when the year was up, the book—which was shaping up to be a lot larger than she initially thought—wasn't yet done.

"I do not entertain the idea of abandonment," she wrote to Gil. Jane was still as committed, if not more, to her ideas but was faced with the problem of money and time. Both were running out.

"We are copying failure," she wrote to Gil. "I am trying to get the theory and practice of city planning and design started on a new and different track."

It was her way of saying, *No, I'm not sending you a draft of my book (yet)*. Gil wanted to see it, but Jane needed more money, time, *and* privacy. She explained that sharing a raw form of her work before she was able to make sense of it would do it a great disservice to what she was trying to accomplish.[2]

Privately, she had deep doubts and periods of confusion about the direction of her work, especially early on in her research phase. She later came to understand that the process of writing and rewriting was her process for thinking through her ideas. Without the false starts and all of the drafts, she couldn't get to a finished product that reflected what she really wanted to say.

The Rockefeller Foundation trusted her process—apparently—as they agreed to fund her work for another year.

And Jane was moved by their unwavering support and faith in her project.

Almost two years after her proposal, she finished the book—twenty-two chapters in total.

As she recalled three decades later, writing the book was a treasure hunt that "lured me into my subsequent life's work."

* * *

The Death and Life of Great American Cities has been called "one of the most remarkable books ever written about the city," and, today, is required reading in most architecture and city planning courses.[3]

As we engage with Jane's most well-known work, we should read it, too, with reservations and skepticism. Some of it feels timeless and relevant. Other passages are out of touch and noticeably silent on a discussion of race and social divisions in her beloved city.

We can value it and grapple with it at the same time.

So why was *Death and Life* so impactful when it was published?

It wasn't just *what* she wrote. The *way* that Jane decided to share her ideas was strikingly different from the way her colleagues were writing about cities. She chose not to use technical terms or jargon that would turn off a casual reader. She wanted both planners and nonprofessional, curious people to be able to pick up *Death and Life*.

You don't need to be an expert to ask the right questions, she insisted in her article for *Fortune*, the seed of her book. "Planners and architects have a vital contribution to make, but the citizen has a more vital one. It is his city, after all."

City-Destroying Ideas

Jane believed that people themselves have the power to reshape their communities, while city planners were very much obsessed with their own ideas.

They were stuck in another time, "clinging to the fashions of their youth," wrote Jane. To her, they were acting like little boys who were captivated by the automobile and a vision of the city built around this exciting new technology. As a result, these men were causing unworkable, disastrous problems for cities and the people who live there.

Modernism is the name for the early twentieth-century art movement that transformed culture, technology, architecture, and city planning across the globe. World War I brought mass death and trauma, but it also brought a dramatic upheaval of what came before. Modernism reflected the idea that the "past" was something "bad"—something to reject. Instead, "progress"—a modern industrial world—was the goal. A new belief in technology was taking hold: The machine would fix all problems. The machine would make lives better and easier.

László Moholy-Nagy was a modernist artist who worked in a whole range of media from painting to photography, film, sculpture, and design. Before he moved to Chicago, Moholy-Nagy was part of the Bauhaus—a group of European artists and thinkers who believed in the power of industry and automation. For modernists like Moholy-Nagy, cars were a sort of mascot of this "vision in motion."

It would be a mistake to think that Jane believed that the modernist movement was inherently bad. She didn't feel strongly one way or another about modernism. "It was just another way of building," she said. So why was she so publicly critical of modernist architects? Why did she devote so much of her book to their "city-destroying ideas"?

City Destroying Idea #1: Break-up the City

To understand the city planners who were so taken with modernism, you would have to go back a bit further in history, Jane explains in *Death and Life*. In 1898, a man named Ebenezer Howard had a plan to "help" poor people in London who were living in crowded and unhygienic conditions. *To fix the city, you've got to get rid of the city*, Jane wrote about Howard's approach.

His idea was to create the Garden City—a series of planned communities on the outskirts of the existing city, where residents could live in one- or two story buildings next to beautiful, green spaces, free of disease, crime, and pollution. Housing would be separated from places where people worked and from recreational activities. Everything would be split up and spread out.

"His aim was the creation of self-sufficient small towns, really nice towns if you were docile and had no plans of your own and did not mind spending your life among others with no plans of their own," Jane wrote, telling us exactly where she stood on this development in the history of city planning.

Howard had enormous influence. Jane acknowledges in *Death and Life* that he spun "powerful and city-destroying ideas." In the 1920s in the United States, a group of professionals, thinkers, and planners called the decentrists took his ideas to heart. Among them was Lewis Mumford.

Imagine this: the city is made up of toy blocks. First, the Decentrists would scoop up all of the pieces that make a city. Then they would sort out the different parts based on use to make their Garden City: housing blocks over here, shopping blocks there, and factories over there.

And the Decentrists were like children, playing a game to suit themselves.

City Destroying Idea #2: A City for Fast Cars
So what did all of this have to do with the modernists and urban renewalists in the cities? In *Death and Life,* Jane explains what happened next, or should we say *who* happened next. The Swiss-French architect, the legend, the modernist: Le Corbusier.

Like the other modernists, Le Corbusier saw industry as the best path forward for humanity. If the car was the machine for moving, the house was the machine for living. He built houses and made plans for cities, including a community in Marseille and a masterplan in Chandigarh, India. He even made drawings of Paris and (thankfully, unrealized) plans that slashed broad sections of the city. *Be gone* to those six-story, cream-colored apartment buildings topped with grey mansard roofs that are as Parisian as croissants—*that's* so *yesterday.*

Jane knew all about these guys, the modernists. Le Corbusier's vision for the city built on the previous ideas of the Decentrists, she explained in *Death and Life.* Buildings with different uses were separated from each other, just like they were in the Garden City. Large green spaces would buffer homes. But there was only one way to make the Garden City vision work in the *actual* city: everything had to be *supersized.*

Instead of building a cluster of low-rise buildings surrounded by big parks, Le Corbusier envisioned ever-repeating, towering skyscrapers in the park—buildings that would house thousands.

He dubbed it the Radiant City, a "vertical garden city."

And the Decentrists absolutely *hated* everything about it. But the Decentrists were a small group with little clout. Le Corbusier got *a lot* more traction. His idealized city was "hailed deliriously" by architects, Jane explained. City planners and builders copied his vision like disciples. The birth of the Radiant City was a significant turning point in the history of city building. We are still today feeling the impact of city building that Le Corbusier ignited.

Roads were built to move traffic quickly through the city. Short streets and blocks (obstacles that would necessitate a car stopping at an intersection) were removed altogether. The new city "was everything in a flash, like a good advertisement," Jane wrote about this new obsession with traffic circulation and speed.

The new city was fast.

The new city was clean.

But was it good for the people who lived in these places?

* * *

Jane's through line in her professional work and activism was all about redistributing power through bottom-up, grassroots community action. Le Corbusier's belief system was the exact opposite of Jane's. To him, the city planner was meant to invoke a godlike power to create his utopia for the masses. "There is a new spirit," he wrote in his *Magazine Esprit.* "It is a spirit of construction and synthesis guided by a clear conception."

For Jane, this was an unacceptable, dangerous approach to placemaking. "The planners of garden cities had it all decided what the meeting should decide, what life should be like for people, what was and what wasn't good for them," Jane said. "This is true of all utopian thinking."

They were looking at an idea of a city on paper. They were looking at the promise of the suburb. They were looking at the pop-up wonder of the great fairs and exhibitions. They were looking at everything and "anything but cities themselves," Jane wrote.

Like the child with blocks who builds his dream city on a whim, "Le Corbusier shouts 'Look what I made!'" Jane writes. "Like a great, visible ego it tells of someone's achievement. But as to how the city works, it tells, like the Garden City, nothing but lies."

A People's Approach to City Building

In 1961, the year that *Death and Life* was published, Jane would have looked out the back window of her apartment on Hudson Street and seen her neighbor, Abram Greiss. A fellow artist, Adam spent his time chiseling large slabs of stone, whittling them into different figures between his shifts at Macy's. Jane crafted her ideas in a similar fashion—laboring over her manuscript for years on her trusty Remington typewriter.

In *Death and Life*, Jane riffs on the kinds of neighborhood places that work to keep the public spaces and sidewalks filled with people—not the *idea* of people that the planners were pushing.

What role should the government play in a people's approach to city building? Jane asks her readers. *There's a problem with housing too—the mass-produced kind is terrible, for starters. And in those places where people need housing, they can't afford it.* She also argues for better public transportation in place of the massive freeway projects that tear through the heart and energy of downtown.

New York is the playground for her ideas, of course, and she pays the most attention to her own neighborhood. But she pulls in examples from cities across the US, including Boston, Philadelphia, Pittsburgh, Chicago, San Francisco, Baltimore, and Washington, DC.

Jane weaves her arguments around ideas that expand on one another—beginning with the front stoop of her brownstone and ending with a broad stroke, big picture idea plucked from the field of complexity science, of all places, and applied to *her* laboratory, the city.

"This book is an attack on current city planning and rebuilding," Jane wrote in the book's opening lines. She told her reader in plain language what they should expect: a book about ordinary and functional urban places. "What, if anything, is a city neighborhood, and what jobs, if any, neighborhoods in great cities do. In short, I shall be writing about how cities work in real life."

So how *do* cities work according to Jane Jacobs? Let's look closely at some of the main themes of *Death and Life* to see what we can value and what we can reject in our reading of her famous book today.

Below we'll look at some of the "city sketches" that Jane offers about her own neighborhood. Then we'll get into the central thesis of her book—how a block works.

The Sidewalk Ballet

Cities work because people work. And play. And love. And fight and chat and hang about with nowhere to go. In the early morning, Jane would emerge onto her "stage" with a broom in hand to sweep the sidewalk just as the chairs were being put out at the café and the market crates were being stacked. The children appeared next, rambling through on their way to school. Jane would inevitably nod to the man selling fruit, as if the entire scene was a choreographed number in a musical. A city block that brings people together naturally is not dull or boring. It is moving, changing, breathing, and evolving. Jane called this daily, unfolding scene the sidewalk ballet—an improvisational rhythm of daily life on Hudson Street.

Street Play

I know Greenwich Village like the back of my hand, Jane's son, Ned, told her. Children played on the streets and the sidewalks out of necessity. It was the outdoor space near their homes. "No normal person can spend his life in some artificial haven, and this includes children. Everyone must use the streets," Jane wrote. Cities are for families.

Adults running an errand, meeting a friend socially, or working a shift would perform their bit part as playground supervisor by admonishing children who were endangering themselves near automobile traffic. When Jane's own son did this, he got a mouthful from Mr. Lace, the locksmith.

But the kids were mostly left alone. One evening after work, Jane counted a dozen children playing before the half-watching eyes of fourteen adults. Children need this opportunity for incidental happenstance and unscheduled play. "They slop in puddles, write with chalk, jump rope, roller skate, shoot marbles, trot out their possessions, converse, trade cards, play stoop ball, walk stilts, decorate soap-box scooters, dismember old baby carriages, climb on railings, run up and down," Jane wrote about the kids who hung out near her doorstep.

Play is not a treat or a bonus. Play builds resiliency and

autonomy. It also helps with self-regulation, writes early education researcher Erika Christakis in her book *The Importance of Being Little*. And the stoop and sidewalk served as an ideal and natural setting for play. "The myth that playgrounds and grass and hired guards or supervisors are innately wholesome for children and that city streets, filled with ordinary people, are innately evil for children, boils down to a deep contempt for ordinary people," Jane wrote.

Street Design and Caregiving

The people promoting this supposedly better city were also making things much more difficult for caregivers. "Men are not an abstraction. They are either around, in person, or they are not," Jane wrote.[4] If the men—who were more likely to work outside of the home in the 1950s—are stocking the shelves of the corner store, tending the bar, repairing shoes, or fixing a pothole, they are also serving as adults on official childcare duty. Separating men who now need to go to work way *over there* means that children lose access to men in their daily life and play.

The Four Ingredients of a Successful City

Does neighborly mutual support, happenstance social interaction, and collective community caregiving . . . just happen? Jane devotes an entire book to trying to answer this question.

Picture it—a child on your block plays ball near your stoop and you watch them while their dad picks up bread

Jane Jacobs, center, at the White Horse Tavern on Hudson Street in Greenwich Village, 1961. CERVIN ROBINSON

for dinner. The owner of the deli stops your mom to tell her about the public meeting he attended last night. Your older brother checks in on an elderly neighbor who missed their evening stroll. These seemingly mundane social interactions form a basis for community reciprocity and caregiving.

City blocks with little housing diversity that are designed around cars and not people (with everything spread apart, accessible only by automobile) stifle human interaction. Without this everyday connection, our collective power for organizing and our very human need for support and mutual aid are diminished.

Jane rejected the kinds of places that divided us: places

where life is depersonalized, each of us in our silos. If we are separate, we don't engage with people who have different political and religious beliefs. We don't talk to people who don't look like us. Jane shines her light on the kinds of neighborhoods that bring us together. A successful working city requires a recipe of moving parts and pieces that work together. They are:

1) Lots of purposes, mixed together in one place

2) Short blocks

3) Old and new buildings mixed together

4) High density of people

Without just *one* of these four elements, the city doesn't work properly, Jane explained.

So let's get into each in detail.

#1. A Place with Lots of Purposes

On Hudson Street, Jane passed factories, brownstone apartments, schools, tenements, shops, corner stores, bars, cafés, and churches on the walk down her block. The structures and physical buildings that allow for lots of kinds of businesses, homes, and services work together like nectar and bees; people are drawn to various establishments at all hours of the day and evening, depending on their errand or reason to be wherever they are. By separating out homes from shops, from bars, and even from schools, architects and planners were essentially segregating people—by race, ethnicity, and income. To avoid the death of a city, we've got to *mix the uses* of buildings in a neighborhood, Jane argued.

#2. Short Blocks

Short blocks expand the number of opportunities for people to get from here to there. Put more simply, this means more connections between places. Streets that are broken up with lots of crossings have the added benefit of being safer for people walking, biking, and rolling too.

#3. Old Buildings

A city block built brand-new in one fell swoop is death. "It becomes a place to leave," writes Jane. Like a mature tree that has experienced more days than many of the humans walking beneath its canopy, the benefits that an old building provides are irreplaceable.

New construction takes money, and lots of it. Who can pay that kind of rent? Well-established, chain store companies that starve existing small-scale businesses. If you don't want the chain store, then try keeping the old buildings. Fix them up, renovate, add to what's already there, sure—but keep them. "Cities *need* old buildings to incubate new enterprises," Jane told a reporter about a decade after she wrote about the importance of old buildings in *Death and Life.*[5] An entrepreneur goes through necessary stages of experimentation and failure. High rents are barriers to their success.

The first-floor retail storefronts and commercial spaces of Jane's Hudson Street building comprised a mix of sole proprietors and mom-and-pop shops: an interior designer of religious spaces, political clubs, musician societies and associates, a mail-order tea salesperson, a watercolor teacher, a tuxedo renter, and a Haitian dance troupe. "There is no place for the likes of us in new construction," she wrote.

#4. High Density of People

Jane's first three ingredients for a successful, working city block have to do with the physical form of a place. The fourth and final ingredient has to do with people; that is, the more people, the better.

The Garden City planners believed that a high concentration of people in a place was unsafe and dangerous. That's why they wanted to create new places outside of the city for people to live and work.

But a high concentration of people is *not* the problem, Jane wrote.

Overcrowding *is* the problem.

Density is the ratio of the number of people in a certain area. Cities = high density. A rural town = low density (of people, maybe not cows).

Overcrowding within homes—whether they are urban, suburban, or rural dwellings—"is almost always a symptom of poverty or of being discriminated against," wrote Jane, "and it's one (but only one) of many infuriating and discouraging liabilities of being very poor or of being victimized by residential discrimination, or both."

Equals Diversity!

So, all together, these four ingredients are a foundation for a successful, working city. Remove one, Jane argues, and the alchemy doesn't happen. The result is flat, stagnant *sameness* instead of a place that welcomes and sustains businesses and homes of people of different races, ethnicities, and incomes. The variety of ideas, perspectives, and experiences is the very point.

Diversity is not simply a nice thing to have. It's a *need*. Nothing less than the long-term sustainability and financial health of a place is at stake. A city's success is directly tied to thoughtful, purposeful planning that cultivates diversity and participation by the people.

More Homes

There are two major problems with housing, Jane wrote. First, we don't have enough of it. Second, the housing that poor people can afford isn't the kind anyone would want to live in. Does the problem of not having enough affordable housing justify the development of instant urbanism by the truckloads? *No way*, Jane argues. Enough with the big projects, she wrote. Unlike the master planners, who were playing a game with people as their test subjects, Jane proposed subsidizing some of the housing so people with limited incomes could live in decent, affordable homes next door to people with greater incomes. Landlords would simply collect the same amount of money regardless of where it came from.

Jane's thoughts on housing in *Death and Life* beg us—her readers from the future!—to dig in and engage more deeply. Jane's devotion to small projects feels like an unsophisticated bandaid for the pressing issues of the twenty-first century. With skyrocketing costs of housing, widespread houselessness, and climate catastrophes that are predicted to trigger mass migrations—it's worth questioning how small-scale projects *alone* can adequately address our global problems today.

Places for People, Not Cars

Building a city to accommodate cars and simply ignoring all of the other stuff—parking, congestion, air quality, less space for people—was looking away from an ugly truth. Vehicles have their place on the city street, Jane admitted. But let's look—really look—at the harm we have caused by welcoming them in droves.

Jane makes a lengthy argument in *Death and Life* for the "attrition of automobiles"—a fancy way to say the "reduction of the number of cars in a place." (The fight for Washington Square Park is a perfect example of making a place less accessible to cars.)

Parking lots, road-widening projects to improve traffic flow, an expressway to connect here to there, new access ramps that connect the fast and slow parts—all of these things bring *more* cars to the city.

How, then, are we going to get anywhere? It's a fair question. While discouraging cars, we need to also make investments in public transportation, Jane argued. When automobile drivers get the advantage on the streets, the riders on the bus lose out. It's not a popular opinion, Jane acknowledges. There are "no funds for it" and "no faith in it."

And what if we can't stop it? The road widening, the expressway-building, the "sacking of cities" by cars? Here, Jane seems prophetic. The last laugh will be on all of us who march toward "progress" in the choking exhaust of bumper-to-bumper rush hour, in our five-ton steel cages, all while the planet burns.

Eyes on the Street

If a city street is used, then a city street is safe, Jane thought. She coined the phrase "eyes on the street" to describe the natural order of the residents, proprietors, and neighborhood fixtures along a city block who ensure public safety and order just by having a look at what is happening outside their door.

Jane argued that the very presence of people in a neighborhood—lots of people, from the shopkeeper to the corner store patrons to the stoop sitters—creates a shared sense of safety. The feeling of knowing your neighbors have your back.

But let's take a closer look at Jane's "eyes on the street" theory.

Jane is describing a narrow and false sense of safety *she*—as a white woman—feels in public space. Her worldview fails to consider the ways race and place intersect.

What about the harm and violence *caused* by surveillance—by American policing and informal, "citizen" policing? Jane's idea of "eyes on the street" doesn't really hold up in the context of America's long history of racist policing—from the "slave patrols" of the 1800s (organized groups of armed men who terrorized enslaved people throughout the antebellum South) to modern day policing. Today, Black people, people of color, and other marginalized groups are more likely to be stopped, harassed, and killed by the police, or by white vigilantes—regular citizens who take it into their own hands to police their neighborhoods in the name of "safety."

The political activist Angela Davis connects the dots between surveillance and white supremacy in public space. These are simply everyday realities in a country with a long history of racism. "The use of state violence against Black people, people of color, has its origins in an era long before the Civil Rights movement—in colonization and slavery," writes Davis in her book *Freedom Is a Constant Struggle*.

Using one example (of which there are many, by design) in modern America, Davis points us to the murder of Trayvon Martin, a Black teenager who had just bought some Skittles from a convenience store in Sanford, Florida. George Zimmerman, a member of the gated community's "community watch," hunted down and killed the boy. Davis highlights Zimmerman's role in the context of America's history as "a would-be police officer, a vigilante" that "replicated the role of slave patrols."[6]

When slavery was abolished, white supremacy didn't just disappear. Something else took its place.

Now, a new system of slavery emerged: arrest and imprisonment. In the American South, Black people could be arrested for loitering—that is, simply standing around. Later, in 1877, Jim Crow laws legalized a racial caste system, with mandated "separate but equal" spaces for Black and white people. In the early nineteenth and twentieth centuries, the barbaric practice of lynching became a common occurrence—white mobs executing Black people publicly for any perceived "slight," including walking down the street.

And all of this was spurred by white America's fear of Black people—the racist (and obviously incorrect) idea that Black communities are dangerous, and thus must be policed.

In the 1940s and 50s, around the time Jane moved to the Village, not much had changed. Redlining and white flight created further disinvestment in Black communities. As a result, crime rose. Guess what happened next?

Instead of ensuring that all people had access to basic human rights and social services, America responded in line with the racist policies of its past. More police—which meant more arrests, more incarcerations, and more police murders, all disproportionately targeting Black people and people of color. And this systemic violence has continued into the twenty-first century. "Young Black males were twenty-one times more likely to be killed by police than their White counterparts between 2010 and 2012," writes Ibram X. Kendi in *Stamped: Racism, Antiracism, and You.* "The under-recorded, under-analyzed racial disparities between female victims of lethal police force may be even greater. Black people are five times more likely to be incarcerated than Whites."[7]

People who were designing cities in the '70s (white men, mostly) developed something called Crime Prevention Through Environmental Design (CPTED), an approach to urban planning that used architecture and environmental design to "prevent crime." *This will make our neighborhoods safer*, the planners thought. *We can make it easier for the police to do their job.* So urban planners went ahead and built things (like street closures, walls, and single points of entry) to control access to places (or in some cases, *took away* things, like street trees). And those things *did* make it easier for the police (and regular citizens) to do their "job." Those things made it easier for the powers that be to surveil, harass, arrest, and even kill people who were deemed "unsafe."

Amina Yasin, an urban planner in Vancouver, calls on planners to end this sort of practice of designing spaces to make it easier for police and residents to "keep watch." CPTED has been used by planners to supposedly reduce crime, Yasin writes. But this only perpetuates anti-Black racism in public space. She highlights the harmful practice of white people questioning the presence of Black people in communal spaces of apartment buildings. She also explains the need for "neighborhood care" (protection of our fellow community members' health and welfare through acts of mutual aid, cooperation, and solidarity)—not neighborhood watch.[8]

Jane wrote a bestselling book with an entire theory around maintaining so-called safety in the streets and on the sidewalks, but what she argues for is a false sense of safety.

Her "eyes on the street" theory is deeply mistaken. Jane doesn't address the harm and violence that surveillance *causes*. She doesn't discuss the ways racism can be traced all the way back to the United States' founding—or how these beliefs became part of our nation's laws and systems. She doesn't discuss how this history informs how people live in America today: who has access to housing, education, jobs, healthcare, the voting booth, and—significant to our discussion here—freedom from policing and incarceration.

Gentrification

Jane writes *a lot* about gentrification in *Death and Life*. But she never uses the word, and for a good reason: it hadn't been invented yet.

So what exactly is gentrification? The British sociologist Ruth Glass is credited with coining the term in 1964 to describe the process of new people coming into a place and displacing the existing residents.

The first outsiders typically aren't ultra-rich. Rather, they are people with creative gigs that pay less who are trying to make it work—so-called bohemian types. They are followed by the "gentry," people of high social status with bigger bank accounts and a history of privilege. In other words, white families who have accumulated generational wealth (cash, property, or investments passed down from their parents or other relatives) suddenly pop up with enough money for a down payment. These wealthier people drive up rent and attract new and different businesses to the area. What usually follows is displacement—residents, some of whom have been there for generations, can no longer afford to live there.

Jane has a lot to say about gentrification. And, confusingly, she offers a good version and a bad version of it.

Stick with me.

Her "good" version is an awkward mouthful: an "unslumming slum," meaning an evolving place that's generating economic growth. A place where local people, new arrivals and long-term residents alike, work together to contribute to their communities. The income from their work (a mom-and-pop shop in the area, for example) is circulated back to the people who live in that place. Sounds really nice. Maybe there are places like this. Are there many, though?

She also had a *bad* version of gentrification that's essentially our working definition of the term today—something she calls the "self-destruction of diversity." (Again with the overly complicated terms.) Here is a place that is negatively impacted by a quick rush of newcomers. It's a place that's becoming homogenous. A working-class place becoming middle-class. A diverse place becoming white. The people who were already living there can no longer afford to stay and are pushed out. *Displaced.*

According to Jane, the newcomers in the Village in the '60s *weren't* negatively affecting the residents who had lived there for longer. And while new residents—like her—smoothly integrated into the community, she insisted that existing residents of the West Village were reaping benefits too, by moving into the middle class.

So Jane's doing this thing where she's (1) defining gentrification, (2) claiming it's not happening where she lives, and (3) gentrifying a neighborhood, all at the same time.

For someone with *so* much to say on the topic, Jane left some big holes in *Death and Life*. Like her theory of "eyes on the street," her idea of "good" gentrification doesn't hold up.

"I know that 'gentrification' is but a more pleasing name for white supremacy, is the interest on enslavement, the interest on Jim Crow, the interest on redlining, compounding across the years, and these new urbanites living off of that interest are, all of them, exulting in a crime," wrote Ta-Nehisi Coates in his book *We Were Eight Years in Power: An American Tragedy*.[9] Coates asks his reader to look at the new city dweller as someone who has benefited from systemic racism, buoyed by the false narrative that white people are superior. He paints a vivid picture of the owners of luxury real estate—happy no matter who continues to lose, transaction by transaction.

Without equal access to quality education, fair wages, the voting booth, good health care, and—significant to our discussion here—the ability to purchase a home and build generational wealth, it's not a fair or accurate telling to claim that *everyone* benefits from an improving place.

There's some irony here. Jane brushes off the role gentrification plays in displacement. And displacement is the very thing Jane Jacobs will spend her life fighting *against*. With a big asterisk: *Jane concerns herself with displacement caused by urban renewal*. She doesn't see—or doesn't choose to write all that much about—the displacement caused by middle class white people moving in, down the block.

Take Rittenhouse Square in Philadelphia, for example.

For Jane, who wrote about the area in the *Journal of the American Institute of Planners*, this was a reinvigorated neighborhood, with steadily improving living conditions. But she doesn't mention the long-term Black tenants who were actively being pushed out by the wealthier white people doing the "improving." Where do the Black tenants of Rittenhouse Square fit into Jane's description of an unslumming slum?

Well, in this example, Black people don't figure in at all.

A People's Vision for Community Building

The planners thought that people in cities were all in need of "saving." But Jane and her neighbors didn't need saving, of course. To Jane, it is the people themselves who hold the power to create the communities that *they* envision. In the final pages of *Death and Life*, Jane describes something she calls "planning for vitality." The big idea that Jane lays out is an alternative to the racist practice of slum removal. Stop kicking people out of their homes. Our city leaders and residents together should be asking questions instead:

How do we empower people to support one another?
How do we make our public spaces safe and welcoming for all?

How do we encourage the growth of neighborhoods that offer lots of reasons for being there?

How do we do more of the things that are working well? And avoid the temptation to do the things that look nice but don't materially improve our communities?

How do we protect the homes of people—"whoever they may be, to stay put by choice"—in order to encourage diversity of all kinds?

Jane argues that *all* of our participation is necessary to plan for our collective future—our financial well-being, our health, and the sustainability of our communities. Government should be focused on supporting neighborhood businesses. Elected leaders should be doing whatever they can to get rid of rules or laws that are barriers to local innovators and entrepreneurs. Instead of approving slum clearance, the city council should focus on igniting the particular talents of people who are already right there, with all of the ingredients necessary for success.

"Consider how much investment in new and young enterprises might be bought with $300 million," she writes in the *Economy of Cities*, referring to the ridiculously high price tag of high-rise, segregated public housing built in East Harlem during the 1950s.[10]

When local investment happens, good things follow, argues Jane. There are more opportunities for expanding wealth. The residents themselves reap the benefits. And when citizens drive decision-making and budgeting, they create authentic attachments and belonging to their community. The people who live there, who use the streets and sidewalks, who create small businesses from their kitchen—*they* benefit.

* * *

But if the story had unfolded like this, well, we could stop here.

The money was spent, all right: it was just spent on the wrong thing, in the wrong way.

It wasn't spent on dismantling racist systems.

It wasn't spent on reparations.

Moses and others who built large, segregated spaces were peddling a story about helping ordinary people. In reality, they were contributing to racial disparity and inequity.

Millions of dollars were poured into bulldozing, destruction, and displacement.

It was spent to benefit the people who already had all of the power.

CHAPTER 8

AFTER THE BOOK

"I don't know who this celebrity Jane Jacobs is—it's not me. My ideal is to be a hermit, to a certain extent, and do my work. . . . You either do your work or you're a celebrity; I'd rather do my work."

—JANE JACOBS[1]

Jane wrote her book for both the people who designed cities and the casual reader, someone without a degree—a regular person. Her presentation was simple, but her ideas were sophisticated and at times quite lengthy. But she never considered condensing the book to make it more appealing to her reader. "My own view is that this country is full of digesters, reviewers, and summarizers, and those who do not care to read a book as long as this will get some of the drift of its ideas through those means anyhow," she said.

When *Death and Life* hit shelves, it was a sensation, marking Jane as an antiestablishment mom, neighborhood truthseeker and prophet, and a force lacking credentials with a sixth sense about cities. "No matter how they like her assumptions, everyone agrees that she has started something," wrote Eve Auchincloss and Nancy Lynch in *Mademoiselle*.

The reviews poured in, and they were glowing. *Death and Life* "is the most refreshing, provocative, stimulating, and exciting study of this greatest of our problems of living which I have seen," wrote Harrison Salisbury in the *New York Times*. "Jane Jacobs achieves a brashly impressive tour de force" wrote another *New York Times* reviewer, Lloyd Rodwin.

Jane took pleasure in the accolades. She enclosed several positive blurbs in a letter to Gil, her champion at the Rockefeller Foundation, along with this postscript: "As an antidote to the praise, I am getting a spate of furiously angry and denunciatory letters from planners and housers who seem to have me tabbed as an irresponsible, if not vicious, demagogue!" She wasn't exaggerating. But you can tell that she took some pleasure in the feather-ruffling.

The response to the publication of the book from experts in her field was in fact deeply divided. The architects were split, but the planners were all in agreement: *They absolutely hated it*, Jane later said. The planners ripped her to shreds, but they probably felt justified. To them, she picked the fight. "It went against everything they'd been taught, and I can understand that," Jane explained. "It's hard to be told by someone: 'Hey, you learned a lot of junk, you should reconsider.'"

They had, of course, been following their new, modernist bible of single-use zoning in cities. And Jane outlined with authority, confidence, and simplicity the devastation that they had inflicted on cities.

The planners' entire professional careers were in question.

Which, of course, meant that the backlash was intense and swift.

"Jane Jacobs has produced 448 pages of bitter, rambling coffeehouse talk," wrote urban renewalist Ed Logue.

Some planners targeted Jane's lack of credentials and gender. "Mrs. Jacobs clearly knows so little about planning," wrote the executive director of the American Society of Planning Officials. In a short blurb, he managed to simultaneously discredit her while questioning her originality. His message to his fellow planners boiled down to: *Well, we knew this all along and have been saying this for years, now. But this lady has come along and now gets all of the credit.*

The harm will be devastating and long-lasting, he told his colleagues—men who needed to be warned of the woman who was doing them all in. "So batten down the hatches, boys," he wrote, "we are in for a big blow!"

Rodwin's review in the *New York Times* acknowledged Jane's outsider status. But he also didn't think that was a good enough reason to criticize someone: "It won't matter that what this author has to say isn't always fair or right or 'scientific.' Few significant works ever are," he wrote.

* * *

"Nothing in America works the same way for blacks and whites," Jane told an audience years later at an Earth Week teach-in in 1970. "I think of how easily and how long white liberals ignored or rationalized away—some still do—the insanities and brutalities of slum clearance, public housing, welfare and urban renewal carried out in the name of abstract societal progress."[2]

Jane was frustrated with white progressive people who couldn't see how or why urban renewal was so damaging. But she herself ignored the problems of institutional racism and inequality in her beloved city.

In *Death and Life*, Jane crafts a story around the importance of the built environment. To her, the physical spaces around us play a very important role in our ability to connect with one another, move around, and function effectively as fully realized social, political, neighborly beings. There were critics who didn't buy it. The planner and author Kevin Lynch wrote that Jane's book was both "brilliant and distorted"—that it "assumes that buildings and streets have a very singular power to change people's lives." The American sociologist Herb Gans thought Jane's greatest work missed the mark. She was "blind to issues of class and race," he said.

Jane's editor, Epstein, had asked her to more intentionally consider the role of race in her book.

If we assume Epstein is asking Jane to comprehensively address racism embedded in American institutions, Jane's response is profoundly lacking: It's "a poor idea for my book," Jane wrote back to him over the Christmas holiday, before the publication of *Death and Life*.

"I don't think that you can proceed as though the question didn't exist," Epstein replied.

But for Jane, the matter was decided. "Do not cherish a hope that I will change my mind because I am very convinced about this."[3]

In the end, Jane got her way. She dedicates little space on the pages of *Death and Life* to systemic racism. Later in life, Jane was more vocal, or knowledgeable, or both. "Worst of all is racial discrimination," Jane said in a 1969 interview, eight years after the publication of *Death and Life*. "It's the very thing that prevents Black people from the benefits afforded to white people, including access to mortgages and small business loans that would allow them to solve problems . . ."[4]

It's ironic that someone who was so critical of urban planners for ignoring actual people had her own significant issues in this area too. "Jane, in short, didn't see what she didn't see," Kanigel wrote a half century after the publication of *Death and Life*. "And what she didn't see . . . was the troubling impact on cities of race, class, and ethnicity."[5]

* * *

Perhaps not surprisingly, given the message of citizen empowerment, the general public embraced Jane's ideas—both liberals *and* conservatives.

Did Jane think that the book had any real influence? Yes and no. To the people who already believed in this stuff, yes. It confirmed what they knew. But she took no credit otherwise. "Occasionally this book has been credited with having helped halt urban renewal and slum clearance programs," she wrote much later, looking back at this moment in history. "I would be delighted to take credit if this were true. It isn't. Urban renewal and slum clearance succumbed to their own failures and fiascos."

Eventually, as the decades passed, even the planners warmed to Jane. But notably, the people in government still hadn't caught up the way planners had, Jane told an interviewer in 2000.[6] They were steps behind the people they served, people who had a far better understanding of what makes their cities work than they did.

By the end of the decade, *Death and Life* was known as a modern classic, included in college classes across the US. Roberta Brandes Gratz, Jane's colleague and friend, wrote about the long tail of *Death and Life's* impact, describing Jane's status as a writer of a "select literary group," an honor bestowed on a handful of thinkers whose books have profoundly changed society, like Rachel Carson with *Silent Spring* and Ralph Nader with *Unsafe at Any Speed*.

"She's entirely original," said Jane's longtime editor, Epstein. "She's not out to destroy other people's ideas. She thinks on her own. . . . She was born differently. She's a genius—that's what a genius is. They're told to think in a certain way and they can't."

* * *

When we think of Jane Jacobs today, it's difficult to describe her achievements and activism without also explaining the larger-than-life force that was Robert Moses. But Moses wasn't really mentioned much in her book. Weird, right?

Jane Jacobs's biographer, Peter Laurence, explained it this way: By 1961, people had already caught on to Moses. He was increasingly known for his destructive footprint on New York and beyond. Jane didn't really have to add to that conversation.

In the archive at Boston College, you can see the single letter that Moses wrote in response to Jane's book.

November 15, 1961
One Gracie Square, New York
PERSONAL
Mr. Bennett Cerf
Random House, Inc., New York
Dear Bennett:

I am returning the book you sent me. Aside from the fact that it is intemperate and inaccurate, it is also libelous. I call your attention for example, to page 131.

Sell this junk to someone else.

Cordially,

Robert Moses[7]

The story of Lewis Mumford and Jane Jacobs, on the other hand, is lesser known and arguably more surprising. Remember, Mumford was Jane's early mentor of sorts. He encouraged her to seek out a mainstream audience. To write *the book*. Their interplay was a dramatic and very public battle of two intellects: one established, older, and male; one emerging, representative of a new generation, and a woman.

Just a few years earlier, he sang her praises in their correspondence. Jane was up and coming, and he could appreciate her vision while retaining his "expert" status.

"Always do what you'd really like to do," he wrote to her in 1958, when they were still on good terms.[8] Jane had positive things to say about his work too. She credited

Mumford as being "one of the first Americans to scent the threat to all community values by what he called the 'insolent chariots'"—that is, *cars*.

But the publication of *Death and Life* provoked Lewis Mumford, and his bitterness was unleashed. Jane was a "confident but sloppy novice," Mumford wrote to his friend in the Department of Political Science at the University of California the same year that *Death and Life* was published. "P.S. This note is not, of course, for publication," he also wrote. For the time being, he kept his scorn (mostly) to himself.[9]

A year later, he worked up the nerve to go public with his disdain. "I held my fire for a whole year, but when I got down to write I discovered that the paper burned, in spite of the long cooling period," he later wrote about his rage for her.

The New Yorker published his scathing review. The gist of his lengthy takedown? *This person is a woman and therefore can't know about serious stuff like city planning.* He referred to her Harvard talk as *Sense and Sensibility* and to *Death and Life* as *Pride and Prejudice*, the titles of two Jane Austen masterpieces. It's a point that makes little sense other than that he meant it to land squarely as an insult, with Jane's gender front and center.

Anyone who goes against her are enemies of the city, he declares. Her handling of the historical bits is "comic," and she is bad at getting her facts straight. Her popularity is "rampant"; her followers are "uncritical."

Any attempt at complimenting his mentee is erased within the same very sentence. Her words are "foolish," like the shrieks of schoolgirls. Even the title of his review, "Mother Jacob's Home Remedies," points to her gender and her bottom-up prescriptions as laughable. When he writes, "She doesn't consider cities a cancer. She likes them," he means it as a put-down.

In 1965—four years after the book's publication—Mumford wrote in the *New York Review of Books*: "Jane Jacobs' preposterous mass of historic misinformation and contemporary misinterpretation in her *The Death and Life of Great American Cities* exposed her ignorance of the whole planning movement." His wounds were seemingly still fresh and immediate.

But none of this was personal to Jane. Mumford "seemed to think of women as a sort of ladies' auxiliary of the human race," she plainly told an audience two years before her own death. He was simply "a man of his time."

It was so strange to Jane that Mumford had once viewed her as his disciple. She was young and friendly to him, and he took that to mean she approved of all of his ideas. He had created a story about Jane in his mind and he was furious when she did not live up to his idea of her.

It's almost as if he knew that her legacy would stand the test of time.

And his would not.

Jane had a glimpse, early on, of her mentor's disinterest

in cities—the very subject of his life's work and expertise—on a shared car ride. "He had been talking and all pleasant, but as soon as he began to get into the city, he got grim, withdrawn, and distressed. And it was just so clear that he just hated the city and hated being in it. And I was thinking, you know, this is the most interesting part."

CHAPTER 9

THE WEST VILLAGERS VS. THE BULLDOZER

"Poor people, Negroes, and businesses on which many livelihoods depend are tossed out of their neighborhoods in the name of somebody's idea of amenity."

—JANE JACOBS[1]

Eleven-year-old Jimmy Jacobs, Jane and Bob's eldest son, was the first to hear about his favorite tree. It happened to be the *only* tree on Hudson Street for blocks—the one *he* had planted with his parents when he was eight.

And now it was going to get cut down.

We're going to lose our tree, he told his mom at bedtime.

What do you mean? It's doing very well, Jane told her son. *I wouldn't worry about the tree.*

I saw them today, he told her. *The men on the street who were measuring. They told me.*

Jane likely understood right away what and who he was talking about. Surveyors had been up and down their block that week. Of course, she and the other Hudson Street residents were curious as to why they were there and had asked directly. *It's just a routine survey*, the surveyors kept saying.

But Jimmy discovered the real reason.

They told you what? Jane asked her son.

The sidewalks are going to be cut back, made smaller. And the tree will have to go.

* * *

Over breakfast the next morning, Jane and Jimmy drafted a petition. They walked down the block to the printing shop to get the petition printed.

Come back in a few weeks and I'll have your order ready, the printer told them.

But the sidewalks will be cut by then, Jimmy said.

The proprietor of the printing shop took a closer look at the flyer. *Where is this happening?* he asked.

Right here—in front of your shop, Jimmy added.

Come back in an hour. I'll have them ready, he said.

* * *

So what was the big deal about losing a few feet of a sidewalk? Were the Jacobses focusing on a minor detail? It's not as if the city was removing the sidewalk altogether. What was the problem?

Five feet was the problem. On either side of Hudson Street, between Fourteenth Street and Houston, the sidewalks were going to get trimmed by five feet in order to widen the road—enough space to add an additional lane.

But these sidewalks served as important buffers between the street and the space where people walked. It's where children played. The sidewalk was a necessary ingredient that moved foot traffic through a lively neighborhood and allowed shop patrons to frequent local businesses.

To lose ten feet "would have been disastrous," Jane said about her family's important fight for a small bit of space. "And you may be sure that more would have been whittled off in subsequent years, too."

* * *

The Jacobs children positioned their table on Hudson Street, on the very sidewalk in danger. They asked their neighbors to sign their petition, one signature to each petition card in the stack. (Here, appearances were everything. A stack of cards looked a lot bigger than a few sheets of collected names.) Jimmy even made the news. "Eleven-Year-Old Sparks Village Civic Effort" read the headline in *The Villager.*

Jane, who made a good tag team with Jimmy, formed an advocacy group. They called it Save the Sidewalks. The petitions weren't enough by themselves, though, to stop the city's plan. What was more important in the end was knowing people in the right places, Jane later explained. From the PTA to local churches, their movement gained community support and even caught the attention of the president of the Greenwich Village Association, Tony Dapolito, a neighborhood fixture himself and owner of a bakery on Prince Street. And it was Tony's contacts in city government who finally put a stop to the road widening.

* * *

Like the battle to Save the Square, this new fight wasn't an obvious, inevitable win for the Hudson Street organizers. In fact, the Jacobses' neighbors thought they were too idealistic for even *trying* to take on the city in the first place.

It's all been decided.

You can't win.

It's City Hall against . . . these kids?

Five feet. It was a minor win in the scheme of things. But it was a glimpse of the larger civic battles ahead. And Jimmy, just like his mom, sparked the campaign by simply observing daily life as it unfolded on his street.

The surveyors were quick to share their plans with a curious boy because, *really, what could a child do?*

But they didn't account for Jane, the mother behind the boy.

Jane, the lady in the neighborhood who got things done.

Jane, now poised to engage in what would be her biggest fight yet: a battle for the whole neighborhood.

* * *

A few weeks after Jane finished writing her book, she opened the *New York Times* to find an astonishing bit of news. Actually, it was more than astonishing. It was dreadful. Her entire neighborhood was going to be destroyed. All of the buildings would be bulldozed—poof, like magic. *It was all to go.* This time, it wasn't a roadway that threatened their homes—it was a supersized housing development called the West Village Urban Renewal Plan, which made it sound like something nice, something that would spruce up the neighborhood. But there was nothing nice about it: fourteen blocks of the West Village would be demolished. Jane could see it all unfold in her mind: *Urban renewal is the way of the future,* the city would falsely claim. The people in positions of power would agree. And anyone who thought otherwise would be dismissed as backward, in the way of progress.

Of course, the newspaper framed it less dramatically. The *Times* reported on a study that was currently underway. A study is innocuous, right? What harm is there in a simple fact-finding mission? Having covered exactly these kinds of developments for years, Jane could read between the lines. First comes the study, then comes the "blight" label. Then it's demolition.

Another detail jumped out at her: the cost of the study was high. This number was relative to the cost of the entire project, Jane knew. When she did the math, she could see what the developers *really* had in mind—the size of their project and what kinds of apartments they were planning on building. The number was *enormous*, which meant that her neighborhood was not only going to be knocked down—it was going to be knocked down for high-rise luxury apartments.

"May I reassure you that there is no plan to destroy the West Village," the mayor's office explained in a letter to one of Jane's neighbors. The note went on to say that in a year or so, once all the boxes were checked, the West Village *might* end up being a great spot for what the city called "desperately needed middle-income housing."

Jane never wanted to spend her time fighting what were, to her, ridiculous fights. She was far more interested in her work—writing—and living her life. She valued her daily routine, relationships, and community in the West Village. She wasn't a celebrity, like some of her neighbors, but she *was* a fixture. She attended both the local Episcopal church and pig roasts with her Puerto Rican neighbors. She shopped at her local market. She met friends for a beer at the White Horse Tavern and shared espressos with her neighbors at the Lion's Head, the corner coffee shop. "She knows everybody there, and everybody knows her," wrote Jane Kramer in a *Village Voice* profile on the neighborhood's "prophet."

The West Village was home.

And her home was about to be disposed of, an entire neighborhood and all the people and businesses and nooks and gathering places put out to the curb.

Jane was dismayed by the news. "It was an ax over our heads," she later said about her neighborhood's plight. There was no time to waste. On the same day she learned of the urban renewal study, Jane made phone calls to her neighbors. Things were even worse than she imagined: the wheels were already very much in motion, she learned.

Two developers, James Felt and J. Clarence Davies Jr., were the face of the campaign to redevelop the West Village. Surprisingly, the plan to tear down her neighborhood wasn't Robert Moses's explicit doing, but Jane figured that Moses was probably behind the project in some way. He was, after all, responsible for the creation of segregated high-density, high-rise housing projects throughout New York City. Jane speculated that David Rockefeller's organization, the Downtown Lower Manhattan Association, also played a key (and strategically invisible) role. "It was the Rockefellers [who] wanted to knock it down," she said.

Regardless of *who* was secretly cooking up the plans, the city wanted large sections of blocks bulldozed—fourteen blocks between Hudson Street and the Hudson River (bounded by West Eleventh, Christopher, Washington, Morton, and West streets). This was all about clearing out space—warehouses, lofts, brownstones, townhouses, and tenements—to make way for a blank canvas. The developers would then be able to build new projects. Meaning: the developers would then be able to make a lot of money.

The repercussions would be irreversible. These were exactly the kind of large-scale projects that were responsible for the economic decline of cities and "the class segregation of the suburbs" that Jane had written about years earlier in *Architectural Forum*.

By the 1960s, a diverse group of people lived in the West Village. Laborers, artists, and others with limited income were slowly fixing up old row and tenement houses.

All of these people would be evicted. And it's not as if they were going to be magically ushered into a brand-new apartment complex. Jane reported in *Death and Life* that only about 20 percent of displaced residents make it back into public housing.

Because of their day jobs, Jane and a few of her neighbors had some insider knowledge on how the developers pulled the rug right out from under people. They learned about the city's motives, what was and wasn't possible legally, and how powerful players worked together in highly orchestrated maneuvers.

Together, they began their crash course on fighting a large-scale developer. They did it out of necessity. Their only other option was getting pushed out of their homes.

It was kind of like flying an aircraft while building it, in the middle of an electrical storm. The city was the force of nature with a long history of wreaking wide-scale havoc.

But the politicians and developers faced a new kind of adversary, one they hadn't really come across before.

The pilot at the controls of the plane wasn't giving up over a little bit of turbulence.

She didn't know *how* she was going to land the plane. But she knew she would land it.

A People's Guide to Activism (Part II): Save the West Village Edition

Jane left us all a great gift in her recollections of this period of her life devoted to community organizing. Like part I of a People's Guide to Activism (in chapter 6), much of what's included here is based on an interview Jane had with the Greenwich Village Society for Historic Preservation in 1997—looking back a good thirty-six years after the fact. Jane's advice is specific to her cause, time, and place, of course. But the concepts she outlined for historians can be applied to almost any grassroots adventure in advocacy today.

#1. Don't get tricked by the propaganda machine.
The city was making their rounds, packaging their messaging into positives that no one could disagree with. *The cleanliness! The pristine new neighborhood! So many new homes!* Of course, they weren't doing any real citizen

outreach, like door knocking. They were on a tour of established associations. "Being bureaucrats, of course, they were very much impressed by organizations," Jane later said.

Norman Redlich—the same Norman who helped Save the Square—caught wind of the lies. (He had a friend on the inside, who worked for the city.) He called a meeting with Jane, Bob, Edith Lyons, and other neighbors. By playing up the positives and ignoring the negatives, the city gave the appearance of transparency while completely side-stepping what was about to go down. It was a wise strategy: there was nothing for anyone to be outraged about. No one would mobilize against them. It was smart, tactically.

But Norman was smarter.

#2. Double-check your footing if you think you're on the moral high ground.

Jane and her friends weren't just facing off with the city. They were facing off with other neighbors and community leaders who believed in their truest of hearts that what the city was doing was morally right. For some, it was the promise of more housing that justified whatever destruction had to happen. "Anyone against this project is against homes for people," they'd say.

The developers and politicians who had money and accolades to gain must have been thrilled to see their supporters defend this savior narrative. (Only *they* had the simple solution to the housing crisis!) There was no room for nuance or critical inquiry.

But Jane deplored this kind of thinking. The "do-gooders" were fixated on the *idea* of helping people. Not *actually* helping people.

#3. Big, established groups can be slow to act. Make a team that is fast and nimble.

Jane quickly mobilized the opposition.

These were all battles in a bigger war. Like Jane, many of the people who were involved had fought the city before. Residents in nearby neighborhoods lent their support too. "People who got seasoned and educated in one fight could use that in others," Jane said. "And even more important, they had gotten to know people who could be helpful in these battles."

A meeting was called.

Like the Joint Emergency Committee to Close Washington Square Park to Traffic, which was created with a focused purpose, a handful of residents formed the Committee to Save the West Village, with Jane Jacobs as their appointed leader.

#4 Get to know an insider.

They got to work right away. Jane and Rachele Wale invited Lester Eisner from the Federal Urban Renewal Administration to the West Village for a tour.

Lester worked for the other side. But now, here he was, walking around the Village with two polite, interested ladies. They toured all kinds of homes. Met all sorts of people. They saw everything: the different sizes and kinds of apartments, the luxury ones and the ones that the city was clamoring to officially label "slums."

Did Lester feel something from this tour? Did he understand the irony of "bettering" a place by ruining people's livelihoods and homes?

Perhaps. But something else happened at the meeting that was far more valuable than Lester's pulled heartstrings.

#5. Know the rules of the game. (Sometimes, they're rigged against you.)

On the tour, Lester revealed critical information about the development process. It's possible that he didn't even know that he was sharing insider information. He probably considered it common knowledge. And that's the thing: it should have been.

Whether it was purposely revealed or not, Jane and Rachele added this new information to their arsenal.

They learned that specific statistics and data would need to be presented as evidence in order to cue the bulldozer. This included everything from pollution to the age and condition of the building, how many people lived in an apartment, noise, and what a property was thought to be worth.

They learned exactly how a place gets designated as a slum.

#6. What's the public hearing for, anyway?
Tell us. What would you like to see happen in the West Village? the planning commission asked in a public meeting.

But Jane and her neighbors didn't fall for this trick. They had just learned from Lester that the public hearing process can be a complete joke. It's more often used *against* citizens, as a tool to move a project along.

"The urban renewers try to cry up citizen participation to save their programs and solve their problems, not solve the citizens' problems," Jane told an audience at the University of Pittsburgh a full year later, when her battle days were behind her.

They are decidedly *not* committed to solving a citizen's problems.

There are certain legal requirements that a city or town needs to complete before implementing a major change (like bulldozing fourteen blocks). One of those required steps is listening to what the public has to say about the change that is coming. *Would the project impact them negatively? Could it cause them harm?* In the case of the West Village development, *would the slum label destroy the livelihoods and communities of the families who were currently living there?*

The answers to these questions seem obvious—yes, yes, and yes.

Tell us. What would you like to see happen in the West Village?
they asked again.

We won't tell you until the slum designation is removed,
Jane and her fellow organizers told them.

"It was hard for people to believe," Jane later said about
the city's deceit. "Was it hard for us to believe? We had to
keep reminding ourselves at every single meeting that we
did not offer any constructive cooperation to the city about
our area—and why—or we would have been done in."

#7. Beware the big promises from your opponent.

The kids in the neighborhood saw them first. They called
them the creepers—the people who were dropping by and
asking a lot of questions. They were hired by the developers
and mainly targeted Puerto Rican families who were longtime residents of the neighborhood. Jane figured that the
city did this to divide people in her neighborhood—using
racist narratives to pit different groups against each other.
The creepers promised a lot of things—like a better home,
somewhere else—that they never intended to deliver.
Meanwhile, they were collecting information to use against
the very families they were pretending to help.

It was all about trust. And the residents of the West
Village had none for the creepers, who were using them
to make a perfectly legal case to take their homes. Instead,
they believed in themselves, and their collective power.

#8. Band together with your allies.

City council meetings aren't exciting affairs, unless you know what to look for. The drama, the feigned interest, the underhanded power plays—it's all there.

An issue is being discussed. The city wants a certain outcome. Council members expect that their opposition will show up to protest. They directly or indirectly reach out to residents or members of their committees. Those people get up and make heartfelt statements in support of their dream project.

The West Village Urban Renewal Project needed champions, so the city planted them. First, they established a fake organization to give the appearance that there were real people who supported the project. Even though there was strong opposition to the urban renewal project, "it looked on paper . . . as if the longshoremen were in favor of it, as if the artists were in favor of it," Jane said.

Maybe these people *were* part of an actual group, but their numbers were small. So Jane, Bob, and her neighbors took to the streets, bars, and churches to form their own counterattack against whatever lies the puppets were peddling.

They worked quickly to organize their own coalition.

A *real* coalition.

#9. Compile the data.

The creepers were busy poking around—gathering facts

and figures about their homes, streets, and neighborhood buildings. Remember, data collection was the first step toward the city's end goal of complete demolition. Put some facts down and then twist them to show what a dump the place is. *Who wouldn't want this all wiped away?*

The city was using data against them—so why couldn't they use data for *their* cause?

Jane's neighbor built an exhaustive survey, documenting West Village landmarks and noting everything from the demographics of residents to the conditions of buildings.

Look, you've got data. Well, we've got data. They presented their findings, proving unequivocally that their neighborhood was *not* a slum.

Of course, the city had no response.

They had their own data that supported their own narrative. And they liked their story better.

#10. Believe in the surprise effect.

Many tactics, strategies, and efforts need to be happening at once. Some will fizzle. Others will coalesce into something bigger, something unexpected.

The survey was a flop with the city. They couldn't care less. City officials were moving ahead, readying the bulldozers with heaps of money promised by the federal government.

Yet Jane described her homegrown book of facts and figures as "worth its weight in gold."

Not to the city, but to the press.

Reporters *love* statistics. Publish a report, and the article all but writes itself. The national media latched on to Jane's treasure trove of data that detailed the real people and real places that would soon be wiped away, for good.

It was a journalist's dream. Regular people take on the government—the kind of news that would keep readers coming back for more.

#11. Tell your target what you're doing.

The city was tight-lipped about everything. It was how they operated. They drafted plans behind closed doors. They plowed through their checklist of legal requirements, hoping to trip up the residents who unknowingly participated in their game.

But the Committee to Save the West Village took a very different approach: full transparency. Whenever Jane or one of her fellow activists learned of a city or meeting or plan, they announced it—loudly. The tactic generally forced the city to deny whatever it was they were doing, which in turn deflated or foiled their scheme.

The city had a survey? Well, the residents had a survey too. They told city officials that they planned on proving, with data, that their neighborhood would not qualify as a slum. They told the police the truth—that they didn't know how many people would show up on the streets at their rallies. "Bluffing is bad strategy," Jane said. "We figured honesty and full exposure was the best thing."

The committee operated on trust. Organizers and vol-unteers were entrusted with the big picture vision and tactical details. Telling the truth was also a practical matter. So many voices, leaders, and residents were involved in the fight. How could they keep any secrets? If everything was hush-hush, how could their coalition be successful?

The city, in turn, couldn't believe that Jane openly revealed her plans. "Being predators, they instinctively depended on deceit," Jane said about her opponents. "Communities have everything to gain and nothing to lose by bringing everything possible into the light."

#12. Ask: How can we get a good photo out of this?
The painted "X" was the mark of death. It meant that a property was marked for the bulldozer.

One of the organizers riffed on this well-known symbol by taping an "X" on the frames of hundreds of cheap throw-away glasses from Woolworths. Crowds of "crossed-out" people caught the attention of reporters, who spread the story across the world, from South America to Europe.

It was an effective stunt. The *Saturday Evening Post*, a mainstream magazine with a national reach, featured the Greenwich Village activists, self-branded for demolition.

This was a new angle: behind every building were actual people—"condemned" people.

Would a story about a building have spread so fast?

#13. Understand that the coalition is bigger than any one person.

The Committee to Save the West Village often gathered at the local bar, the Lion's Head. Leon, the proprietor, was a useful point person as the owner of a "third place"—a semi-public space outside work or home.

Jane's dining room table served as yet another outpost for organizers. When the Jacobses' light was on at 555 Hudson Street, neighbors knew that they were welcome to drop in to discuss plans.

"Naturally everybody had to work. We all had jobs and some of us who were working mothers had two jobs, in effect," Jane said. "Either their second job or their third job was saving the neighborhood."

It was never *just* about Jane, even though her growing celebrity was a fixation for the city, who strategized on how to take her out. "They thought I was some kind of a witch or whatever," Jane said. If the city could just remove her—take her down—they could topple the entire movement. At least that was their thinking. But the city misunderstood the real strength of their organizing: their collective advocacy.

#14. Flex your spy skills.

A young man named Barry Benepe took a job as a creeper. He was hired by one of the developers who was hoping to make money off the West Village once it was declared a slum.

Jane, as chair of the Committee to Save the West Village, recalled receiving an odd letter from Barry.

What the letter said was far less important to Jane than *how* it was typed.

Every "R" that was printed hung low. This mysterious dropped "R" was the very same typewriter flaw that appeared in all of the typed materials from the made-up community groups that were supposedly in favor of their own destruction.

As the story goes, Jane knew a guy at Columbia University who made a connection between the letters with the dropped "R" and a woman who used to operate a shady business selling term papers to Columbia University students.

This woman was back in business again, apparently.

But Jane had to see for herself.

She pretended to casually drop by her office and, sure enough, *a telegram from Barry was laying out on this woman's desk!*

At this point, the story reads like a *Scooby-Doo* episode. You can almost imagine Jane's delight at her discovery: Could it be that the typist for the developer also happened to be the secretary for the fake community organizations that were pro–wrecking ball? Jane knew that it wasn't a coincidence. But they couldn't just walk into a hearing with some harebrained accusation.

They'd look like amateurs.

#15. Hold a press conference.

Jane's hunch had to be corroborated. She hired a forensic expert—the kind that would testify in trials.

The expert agreed: all of these documents were generated by the same office. But this new information wasn't some grand revelation to the organizers—they already knew full well that the developers and the city were scheming against them. They didn't need any more proof.

And there was no way that the city was going to look at this discovery and see anything other than a bunch of people with too much time on their hands. *So what?* the city would say.

But the newspapers would say the very opposite: *Tell me more.*

So Jane made a big show for the media. On a fall morning in 1961, she held a press conference near City Hall.

These people—the ones who were supposedly in favor of their own demise—they were all planted by the developers.

The public needed to know the truth.

And Jane lifted the curtain.

#16. Disrupt.

While Jane held her press conference, her fellow organizers were around the corner at City Hall, protesting the planning commission.

Inside the boardroom, the city was ready to make it official. They were in the process of requesting $350,000 in

Jane Jacobs holding up documents at a press conference of the Committee to Save the West Village, Lions Head Restaurant, 1961. *NEW YORK WORLD-TELEGRAM* AND *SUN* NEWSPAPER PHOTOGRAPH COLLECTION, LIBRARY OF CONGRESS

federal funding for the urban renewal study. Even with all of the community-led surveys proving the very opposite—the neighborhood was being designated as a slum.

Extra cops were called in. The mood was tense.

The West Village Committee wanted their chance to speak—to show the city that Felt was ramming this slum designation through without public process or input.

But no one on Jane's side was allowed to comment, so one of the attendees yelled out: "Felt made a deal."

"Remove that man!" Felt called to the police.

While he was being dragged out, another resident said, "Felt made a deal!"

He, too, was shown the door. More attendees followed suit. Anyone who tried to speak was removed. Officers shoved protestors on their way out.

The news coverage was unsympathetic: The *New York Herald Tribune* called it a "near-riot." The protestors had "hot tempers" and were "wild," "disgraceful," and "disorderly."

Sure, it was messy. But the time for civil negotiation had passed. Instead, organizers engaged in nonviolent direct action. By yelling out and creating a ruckus, they were stalling the vote.

#17. Whatever you do, don't stop.

If Jane and her fellow organizers folded as soon as they discovered that the city wasn't budging, they would have relinquished their homes to the bulldozer. But as any visitor to the West Village knows, the historic and storied neighborhood pulled through.

They won the battle because they proved, once and for all, that the developer made bald-faced lies, staging fake community groups at public hearings.

But they also won because of their book of stats and

data—a bible of information demonstrating that the people of the West Village, their homes, and their livelihoods had intrinsic worth and value.

Something else turned the tide too: the national audience of onlookers who were curious about those offbeat Village people. Jane and her friends successfully used the press to magnify the actions of money-hungry men in power.

And there was the lawsuit that Jane Jacobs filed against the City of New York.

It was not one but *all* of these actions, taken together. And more significantly—the community effort was sustained and unrelenting.

These people are too excitable, Mayor Wagner told Felt. *They're not giving up.*

Give me one more chance, Felt begged the mayor. *I can appeal to them—once and for all, on their terms.*

#18. When they offer you the bait, don't take it. (You're close.)

The mayor agreed. Felt had one more shot to try to silence Jane and her committee, once and for all.

Felt set up a private meeting with community leaders. He wanted to show them that he was reasonable, courteous, and that his ideas for "fixing" the neighborhood were worth getting behind.

But there was one requirement he insisted upon for the meeting: The Jacobses were *not* allowed to attend.

*   *   *

Chances are, Felt didn't really think he was helping others with his urban renewal scheme. He was probably far more interested in making money, and lots of it.

But it's likely that he *did* believe in the power of his own spin. The do-gooders who were on his side believed they were helping others. So why couldn't he convince some of the other community leaders as well?

Jane and Bob would *never* come around to his side—he knew this. If they attended, he could never successfully make his case.

When the meeting without the Jacobses was called to order, not a single resident budged on their position. They weren't having it, and they wouldn't dream of saying a word about what they wanted instead—they weren't going to be tricked into providing the developers with a public comment.

Jane Jacobs was not there in the flesh.

But her ideas were front and center.

*   *   *

The long working suppers with neighbors after work, the lost sleep, the fear of losing one's home—it was a tiring year, but it was what they were called to do.

Jane, for one, wouldn't have had it any other way. "I mean, we'd all love to have missed having the problem," she said, "but as long as we had it, we wouldn't have missed fighting and winning it. No question about that."

By the fall of 1961, even Felt was done. He could no longer support the West Village project.

And with that, the West Villagers won.

There was still the work of getting the slum designation legally removed. (It would take a few more months.) But the politicians had given up. The developers had given up.

Meanwhile, Jane and her neighbors stood their guard. "The local alert is still on," wrote Brooks Atkinson in the *New York Times*. "The thousand eyes of Hudson Street are watching."

CHAPTER 10

BUILDING HOMES
FOR PEOPLE

"The kind of housing that is most needed and is
already in shortest supply [is] moderate and low cost
housing . . . To neglect new construction within the
built-up part of cities and to concentrate instead . . .
on large vacant sites at city outskirts or in satellite
suburbs is not an answer. The fact is, built-up parts of
cities do need new construction."

—JANE JACOBS[1]

The battle for West Village was a battle of resistance. Jane
and her neighbors fought hard against the terminal diag-
nosis of "slum." And they won.

But it was also a fight that was *for* something. "It's very
hard to be negative all the time and our neighborhood was
full of constructive, non-negative people," Jane said.

Some of her neighbors tried to shame her for being
against more apartments. But they did this all while
glossing over the fact that hundreds of families would
have lost their homes. Over eighty businesses would have

shuttered. And the new isolated high-rise housing wasn't an improvement. "Nobody cared what we wanted when they built this place," a tenant of an East Harlem housing project explained in *Death and Life*. "They threw our houses down and pushed us here and pushed our friends somewhere else. We don't have a place around here to get a cup of coffee or a newspaper even, or borrow fifty cents. Nobody cared what we needed. But the big men come and look at the grass and say, 'Isn't it wonderful! Now the poor have everything!'"[2]

Jane thought there was another way to house people. She wanted to add homes to a neighborhood *without* having to kick anyone out.

Today, a charming railroad track-turned-green space, the High Line, runs through the West Side of Manhattan along Eleventh Avenue. This touristy slice of parkland is not without its own complications, however. At its landing pad to the north sits Hudson Yards, gigantic luxury apartments mixed with global chain stores. It is basically the most anti-Jacobs use of city space imaginable.

In the early 1960s, decades before the High Line and a half century before Hudson Yards, railroads were used for shipping less and less. (America's Interstate Highway System definitely had something to do with this.)

Just south of the High Line, a portion of the elevated railway track ran into the West Village along Washington Street.

It was here—in the grassy, abandoned swaths of land that checkered the edges of the old railroad—where Jane saw an opportunity.

Her idea was novel: build community-driven housing that's truly affordable, doesn't displace, and replicates easily. By filling empty, unused space with new homes, she'd add housing without evicting the residents who already lived there. Not only that, but it was much cheaper to build *her* vision than the developers' (who were interested in maximizing their return on investment). The money that the city was planning to pour into their destructive plan could be used instead across multiple neighborhoods.

Jane had fleshed out her ideas about adding more housing in *Death and Life* just months earlier. Add to the diversity of a place, she wrote. Don't take stuff away. Mix the new with the old.

This was her opportunity to take her intellectual arguments out of the abstract and into reality. And it was the very opposite of the city's overcomplicated, expensive, and destructive approach to building. The moral thing to do happened to also be the most practical thing to do.

"It's not hard to do things right," Jane said decades later. "It's much harder to do things wrong."

* * *

The city, of course, hated Jane's idea, which she called "spot-redevelopment." How could *these people*—ordinary people—take on the work of a developer?

First, with a committee. (Always with a committee.)

The newly formed West Village Committee effort was community-driven. They launched neighborhood surveys, held public forums, and hired an architect. Community needs drove their vision.

Let's be clear—this group was *not* trying to preserve a place under glass, as some have incorrectly gone on to interpret Jane's mission and legacy. The West Village Committee published a plan in 1963 summarizing their aims. They wanted simply to add housing without displacing any residents. In 1961, Jane wrote about "a city's irreplaceable social capital." If anything, *this* was her preservation effort: the network of individuals that makes a community.

"Not a single person—not a single sparrow—shall be displaced" was the motto that was typeset in the booklet advertising the proposal for the new housing. But it was only half the story. Jane wanted an entire new flock of sparrows to join her, adding nests here and there, wherever there was room to tuck one in.

* * *

The new low-rise apartments would fit into the existing community alongside the old buildings that were already there. They would be built at roughly the same size as the buildings already in the neighborhood, and use the preexisting streets without needing to build new ones. More or fewer of them could be added, depending on lot size and availability.

All of the empty lots that were available came in different sizes, just like the families who would soon live there. The architects designed with this challenge in mind.

For people who stood to make a profit on building homes, it wasn't worth it to build something like Jane was building, when they could instead charge a lot of money for new fancy apartments. But the cost of faraway, high-rise housing was a one-way street to segregation, Jane knew. These projects were failures that "drastically affect[ed] the everyday lives of many people, especially children," she wrote.

* * *

The West Village Houses faced problems from the very start. The historian Roberta Brandes Gratz later called the plan "too radical for its time." What could have been a community blueprint was a bit of a community nightmare.

The process took years, and the project was riddled with roadblocks, cost increases, and hoops that the city made the novice developers jump through. In the end, the West Village Houses were built in 1974—a full decade after the initial plans were drawn up.

From a design standpoint, many sacrifices were made from the original, community-driven plan. (And many people thought that the buildings were *really* ugly.)

But some things from the original plan did make it into the end product:

* The new apartments fit the size and shape of the neighborhood.

* The way the apartments were laid out encouraged views of outdoor spaces at all times.

* The buildings were elevator-free walk-ups.

* There was space for a commercial shop on the first floor for tenants' use.

* Parking was tucked away on the street or underground, and not on the property itself.

It was a remarkable accomplishment, even with all of the hang-ups. Over seven hundred community members worked together to build four hundred units of housing, financed with public money.

The apartments "rented like hotcakes" wrote Mary Perot Nichols in *Apartment Life* magazine. A reporter covering the opening ceremonies described the significance of the new buildings that "marked the first time a community group has fought for and achieved the kind of neighborhood renewal that it wanted, rather than having a plan forced upon it by the city."

Today, the houses still stand (despite a teardown threat residents faced in 2017). And they're still affordable, attainable housing in a neighborhood that has otherwise gone on to be largely inaccessible to anyone but the extremely wealthy.

This kind of "spot-redevelopment" is called infill housing today. It is a development approach that is praised and used by community leaders who are committed to adding homes to places in desperate need of them. Unlike urban renewal, infill housing began from a very different starting place. Whereas the modernists and the people who worshiped them wanted to throw it all away and start over, Jane knew that "there is no new world that you make without the old world."

CHAPTER 11

THE PEOPLE VS.
THE HIGHWAY

"There are some people who prefer to travel by
automobile—no matter what. They love what Marshall
McLuhan calls the 'one-ton metal cocoon.' Okay. No
one is making them get out of their cars if they want
to be in them. But they have to accept some of the
disadvantages of travel by car in the city. They make
their own choice. But the point is that the city should
not be remodeled for cars."

—JANE JACOBS[1]

On the evening of April 4, 1968, Jane Jacobs likely learned
of Martin Luther King Jr.'s assassination on the CBS
Evening News, as Walter Cronkite reported it live. In the
week following MLK's murder, protests erupted in over one
hundred cities across the nation.

Among other things, the uprisings pushed President
Johnson to work quickly to pass the Fair Housing Act—
the last of the major Civil Rights–era reform bills. This
law prohibited discrimination (based on race, religion,

nationality, or sex) related to the sale, rental, or financing of housing.

It might be convenient for us today to view the Civil Rights movement as a popular cultural shift that was accepted and embraced by the majority of Americans. But in 1964, according to a Gallup poll, only one in four white southerners approved of the Civil Rights Act, which prohibited discrimination based on race, ethnicity, religion, sex, or country of origin. Only six out of ten of white Americans outside of the South approved. And almost all Black Americans (96%) approved of the new laws. The broad strokes of history can make these movements seem inevitable in retrospect, but in the 1960s, white Americans were split on whether they could even support civil rights laws.

As milestones in American history go, the Fair Housing Act was more symbolic than impactful. The reality was that mortgage discrimination and redlining persisted. Loans were outright refused to people in certain low-income areas; that is, the neighborhoods marked on a map to show where not to invest—where more Black people, people of color, and immigrants lived. The government continued to approve the designation of entire neighborhoods as uninhabitable slums to be cleared, making way for the dreams of a few powerful white men at the top.

Speaking of which. By that time, Robert Moses had begun actualizing his vision: freeways crisscrossing the entire city and monstrous real estate developments laid over entire neighborhoods. "You would see this piece of it and that piece of it, and it wasn't paranoid to think that it was an overall plan that the public really didn't know that much about," Jane later said. "Somebody had a great vision of how New York was to be."

The Washington Square Park roadway that the West Village residents had successfully fought off was part of Moses's master plan. "He would build a bridge without saying there must be a highway at either end," Jane explained. "Or he'd build a road and say nothing about a great big bridge that would be needed."

His projects were seemingly random, bubbling up here and there.

If the interchanges and access roads were like isolated brush fires, Lomex (**Lower Manhattan Ex**pressway), was the inferno that would light the city up.

* * *

Moses's proposal for Lomex, a $100 million ten-lane highway, would obliterate downtown. Two thousand families would be removed from their homes. Eight hundred businesses would close their doors. Ten thousand people would lose their jobs. Over four hundred buildings would be demolished.

"Today our greatest single problem is tenant removal," Moses said about the people who were in his way. "The tendency on the part of people in politics as well as those who are living on these rights-of-way who are immediately affected is to assume that the people who are doing this job are unsympathetic. They're even sadistic. Well, of course, that isn't the truth at all."

Well, of course, that was *exactly* the truth. There was no tiptoeing around it: the project was massive, destructive, and Moses's will for pushing it through was relentless. It was an on-and-off battle, with seeds of the design going as far back as the 1920s. The City Planning Commission approved Moses's proposal for a "crosstown connection" in 1941, a full two decades before plans accelerated to build out the highway. It reared its ugly head again throughout the '60s—first in 1962, again in 1965, and finally in 1968.

This wasn't just some pipe dream: Moses had already proven that he could tear a community to shreds, having "successfully" sliced through the Bronx with the Cross Bronx Expressway.

And now he set his heart on doing the same to Manhattan.

The idea was to create an elevated, fast route for cars that would cross the southern portion of the island. The looming, dystopian megastructure was designed to connect the Holland Tunnel on the West Side with the Williamsburg and Manhattan bridges on the East Side.

Jane wrote about Lomex back in the early '60s in *Death and Life*. It was a "spaghetti-dish of ramps" and a "dumper" that would only bring more cars into the city, demolishing entire neighborhoods in its wake, including the racially, politically, and ethnically diverse areas of Tribeca, SoHo, Little Italy, Chinatown, and the Lower East Side.

It was clear that Moses didn't care about who was in his way. "What I try to do in New York, what we've done successfully in other places . . . is to pay more money to people in cash," he said. "Come take the money and go away. You got people who rent. They don't own anything. What difference does it make when you're talking about an expressway that costs 84 million dollars?"

To Jane, Moses's vision of progress was the driving force of his plans. The displacement of thousands was simply the cost of doing business. *Nobody would take on something so massive and time-consuming just to get rid of something or someone*, she wrote.

Whatever his intent, that's exactly what his highway did.

Moses and his friends in high places who lent their unwavering support (including David Rockefeller and the Downtown Lower Manhattan Association) were *really* pro-highway. And they were skilled at recentering the conversation to justify all the destruction that would unfold. Their talking points were slick and consistent. Driving would be faster and less congested, and the city would boom, they claimed. Real estate values would skyrocket, padding the city's revenue through tax collection.

The great irony is, of course, that they didn't even make things better for the white flight suburban crowd, cruising into the city. And real estate values? You had to be kidding. Urban highways were urban death sentences. Businesses were crippled. The threat of the bulldozer was like a kiss of death—who would invest where a highway would soon be?

* * *

How could this be happening? wondered Father Gerard LaMountain, a priest from the Church of the Most Holy Crucifix on Broome Street.

He was worried. *Really* worried.

His church, his parishioners, their homes, their community—it was all going to get wiped away. The construction on the highway was about to begin.

But it was not for his lack of trying to stop it. He was trying. His parishioners were trying. But something else needed to be done.

They needed help.

The priest paid his first visit to Jane Jacobs sometime in 1962, around the time she had left her job at *Architectural Forum* to write full time. Things were going well for Jane. "I wanted to work on my work," she later said about this time. "I had a feeling the City was making not only my life, but everyone's life, absurd by making us spend our precious time and our energy responding to things of this kind instead of doing the work that we wanted to do."

Father LaMountain knew who Jane was and what she

was capable of. "She has turned her causes into hot-potato issues and is lately the terror of every politico in town," said the *Village Voice* newspaper. "She has mustered public support and sympathy to the extent that even the Mayor bends to a Jacobs decree or completely loses face."

And Jane felt for Father LaMountain. Really, she did.

But to sign up for a fight that was even bigger than the last one?

She couldn't. It was just too much.

"I was reluctant," said Jane, who had just finished fighting off urban renewal in the West Village. "I had put in a horrendous year."

But the priest was persuasive.

She wouldn't join him. But she would offer her advice.

Advice became action, and soon, action would become leadership. It was a slippery slope for someone who wanted to reclaim her time, but Jane Jacobs couldn't stand sitting on the sidelines.

She had, not surprisingly, gone from no to yes overnight. She was in.

* * *

Like the West Village fight, the battle began by getting together all of the people who had a stake in things. Jane formed a committee: the Joint Committee to Stop the Lower Manhattan Expressway.

Their efforts attracted business owners (like Hy Harmatz of the restaurant Ratner's) who would lose their cafés and storefronts. Familiar characters returned—including Assemblyman Louis DeSalvio and activist Rachele Wall, who'd helped in the West Village fight. New allies joined the force as Moses expanded his targets into multiple neighborhoods across Manhattan.

By the mid-'60s, a new awareness around the preservation of historic buildings was starting to emerge. Jane herself joined activists to protest the demolition of the original Penn Station. Their efforts to save the Beaux Arts beauty weren't enough—it was demolished in 1963. But two years later, the Landmarks Preservation Law passed in New York City. The year after that, a national register of historic places was created. The loss of the station was a watershed moment. The station was gone, but something was different after it fell. People seemed to care about these old buildings. Now, the Landmarks Preservation Commission brought increased attention to buildings in the path of Moses's bulldozers. Historic churches, schools, firehouses, and ordinary, everyday buildings like housing, shops, and markets, would all be wiped out.

Margot Gayle, a Greenwich Village resident and an early advocate for SoHo architecture, joined the effort. She gave the Joint Committee to Stop the Lomex an education on preservation. Here was someone who understood the history of the cast-iron buildings of SoHo and made a case for keeping them at a time when there was almost no interest in their architectural worth or beauty. (A decade later, she went on to become the person responsible for SoHo's landmark status.)

Education was one strategy. But there is never just one tactic in a successful campaign. The joint committee understood that they had to make a spectacle in order to capture the attention of the press. They had to spread the word.

One summer evening in 1962, Jane staged a mock funeral march along Broome Street, holding up signs that read "Little Italy—Killed by Progress" and "Death of a Neighborhood."

The visual artist Harry Jackson who drew the skulls and coffins on the signs also happened to be the person who connected Bob Dylan and Jane. Harry got Dylan and Jane together so Dylan could write a protest song for their movement. While some historians doubt that the meeting ever happened, Jim Jacobs (Jane's son) attributes the creation of the song "Listen, Robert Moses," to their brief collaboration:

> Listen, Robert Moses, listen if you can,
> It's all about our neighborhood that you're trying to condemn
> We aren't going to sit back and see our homes torn down
> So take your superhighway and keep it out of town"

The Jacobses spent many evenings together relishing spirited protest songs on the record player. According to Jim, it was Jane who taught Bob Dylan all about how a protest song is structured. As far as we know, Dylan never performed the song for an audience. But there was another public gathering that was taking shape, a public hearing that would determine the fate of the expressway and their homes. It would be their opportunity to lay it all out, but they needed someone who was respected and skilled enough to lead them through the hearing.

Father LaMountain was exactly that kind of person. He was a natural leader who would act as MC of the event, guiding the conversation with the ammunition they had carefully stockpiled.

Their homework was done and they were ready, but life had other plans for the priest. The night before the hearing, Jane's phone rang. Father LaMountain's friend in Massachusetts was very sick. He had to leave town immediately. It was the kind of news that hits you right in your stomach. It was terrible timing for their cause, but of course, he had to go.

With the priest now gone, they had to think quick.

"Somebody else could have [stepped up], but, you might say, I drew the short straw," Jane said about her emergency appointment as the stand-in leader.

Like her entrance into the fight, it was a moment where doing what was necessary outweighed whatever personal feelings she might have had about taking on a leadership role in yet another political battle.

The choice was obvious to everyone, if not Jane herself.

Of course they chose her.

* * *

At the hearing, Jane introduced the speakers, added commentary on their roles, and took care to clearly communicate what was at stake. The meeting became raucous, but not in the way that you might think. It was *joyous*. Congressman John Lindsay showed up, which made Jane and her organizers break out in roaring applause. (He was one of the few politicians who opposed the expressway.)

Mayor Wagner and the board looked on. What *they* saw was an organized, massive neighborhood coalition of voters against a single issue.

They had to make a call.

Would it be a decision based on what was best for their constituents? Or would it be a calculated, political chess move to suit themselves and their own reelection?

They made their ruling.

Wagner and the Board voted *against* the expressway.

In the *NY Daily Report*, Wagner explained his reasoning behind the decision. The highway would have hurt not only the people who would have lost their homes but also the people who would become new next-door neighbors to a freeway.

The group of thirty activists waiting outside City Hall was ecstatic: they hugged and kissed when they heard the news.

It was a day for celebration.

They had won.

* * *

"Dear Mother, We won! Isn't it marvelous! Tell John and Pete, won't you. Much love, Jane," wrote Jane on the clipping of the news article she sent to her mom, proudly announcing their victory.

A few weeks later, in December 1962, the *Village Voice* published a feature on Jane. In no uncertain terms, Jane had soundly defeated the city, "burying Robert Moses" and his highway, they said.

But the traffic commissioner had a different take. Jane was an unhelpful disruptor. In an interview on a TV show in the last week of 1962, Henry Barnes made fun of Jane, calling her a "Jeanne d'Arc protecting the people of the city." Barnes described her on air as an angry, negative woman who stood in the way of progress—"in years to come she will be known as the one who has done the most to keep New York from progressing."

The initial media reports painted the picture of a fight put to rest. But the reality of what was happening behind the scenes doesn't always match up with what is said, or done, in public.

This brushfire had the appearance of being put out, but the embers were still very much burning in the dark.

Local politicians drew their lines. And they were very good at upholding the status quo—to a point. That point was their own survival. They weren't going to be voted out by a bunch of activists on a single hot-button issue. So they folded, giving their voting bloc a win.

Lomex was far from over, however. Not only did the planning commission double down to renew the development of the ten-lane highway, but the State Highway Department and the Rockefellers also became master puppeteers in the planning efforts for Lomex.

But that wasn't the only powerful player who pulled strings behind the scenes.

Sometime before the winning decree, the priest had been called to a meeting by higher-ups in the Archdiocese of New York.

According to Jane, who retold the story in an interview later in life, a monsignor had given the priest an ultimatum. He was told that he must withdraw from this political battle, or lose his priesthood.

It might seem nonsensical, that a priest shouldn't be permitted to vocalize his opposition to a project that would physically destroy his church and dissolve his congregation.

But sense did not play a role in this unseen battle of political power, now in cahoots with religious leadership. The monsignor could not have made himself any clearer. If Father LaMountain wanted to remain a priest, he had to comply. "He really had no choice," Jane said sympathetically about her friend, who, it turns out, never drove to Massachusetts to support his sick friend.

(There was no sick friend.)

The priest had lied to Jane, to his parishioners, and to his friends.

He took his marching orders from the Roman Catholic Church.

And the Roman Catholic Church took *their* orders from Robert Moses.

* * *

The interstate highways that were responsible for choking cities to death in the '50s and '60s weren't just a New York problem: these freeways snaked through cities across the United States. The decimation was real.

Congress began to wake up. They started drafting laws to rein in the powers of developers and politicians who were causing irreversible damage to cities. The 1968 Federal Highway Act, signed into law by President Johnson, would now require cities to relocate families displaced by urban highways into decent housing.

Around the same time *Death and Life* was published, Rachel Carson's book *Silent Spring* hit bookshelves and became an instant bestseller. It was a call to citizens to recognize their impact on the natural world. In the years since the first Lomex battle, more people in American cities began to take notice and express concern about humans' relationship with the earth. With Johnson's new legislation, developers and city officials would be forced, too, to hold multiple public meetings to explain all of the ways that these highways would impact the environment, people, and businesses.

These new protective laws were coming. The pro-highway people knew this, and were racing against the clock to get Lomex approved. The last thing they wanted was to be on the hook for spending more money on affordable housing, or to get hung up in public meetings where ordinary people could discuss the city's polluted air or their bulldozed homes.

* * *

Spring in New York brings out the very best of the city—good weather, flowers in bloom, early evening strolls. As Jane and two hundred residents filled the seats of the Seward Park High School on an April evening in 1968, they must have felt as if the beauty of the season was more fleeting than ever before. All of this—the cobblestone streets, the stoop chats, the corner grocer—would be gone in due time.

The New York State Department of Transportation (DOT) called the meeting at the high school in order to check the box on the "public" part of their requirement. Representatives from Albany sat on the stage. John Toth, representing the State DOT, led the show. The citizens sat below, in auditorium seats, with Jane in the very back. It was very clear who had the power in the room. The people holding power were voted in by the citizens of New York, sure, but the politicians weren't acting like public servants.

When it was finally time to take comments from the floor, people began to speak in favor of Lomex. The State planted their puppets early. But there were hundreds of people in attendance who lined up to speak out against it. They took turns at the microphone, describing the devastation this highway would wreak on them.

There was nothing democratic about the order—or rather, disorder—of the meeting. Officials refused to answer questions. People in opposition to the expressway were interrupted and dismissed. The police loomed over the crowd.

The whole thing was a mess. Jane could tell that it wasn't working. No one was listening to them. She could already see it: the meeting would end, and the developers would check off another box that moved them closer to making their highway a reality.

The crowd felt it too. They needed a catalyst. They needed to flip this thing upside down.

"We want Jane. We want Jane," they chanted.

"I didn't know what to do," Jane said. But something had to be done to bring this thing down.

She took the microphone.

She told them all what a joke this was—*We are even talking to ourselves, with this microphone facing the audience*, she exclaimed.

A politician jumped up and turned the microphone to face the stage.

Jane turned it back. *We have been talking to ourselves so far, so we might as well continue,* she said.

You're just a bunch of errand boys, she then told the politicians. *Well, we have a message for you to take back to Albany: we will never stand for this expressway.*

"What kind of administration," she continued, "could even consider destroying the homes of two thousand families at a time like this? With the amount of unemployment in the city, who would even think of wiping out thousands of minority jobs?"

Jane's next move was surprising, perhaps even to her. She called on the hundreds of community activists to join her on the stage in a silent demonstration. Her intention was simple: to upend this joke of a public hearing that had devolved into a colossal waste of time.

They needed to use their bodies—they needed to march.

Frances Goldin, the Lower East Side activist and preservationist, was the first to join her. Together, they took the stairs to where the officials were seated.

You want to take something back to Albany? Jane thought. *Take* this *back to Albany.*

Jane asked the room to join her. Fifty fellow protestors rose up in solidarity, filing behind the DOT and the city politicians.

"You never saw people so frightened," Jane later said about this moment.

But what happened next was unexpected. No one could have planned it if they tried.

The notetaker who operated the stenotype machine, a kind of specialized typewriter, became terrified. She was hired by New York State to make a record of the hearing, which meant that she had no political alignment with them, necessarily. She likely owned her machine and was scared, for whatever reason, that protestors were going to break it and damage her ability to make money.

"It was her tool," Jane later said about the stenographer. "I, for one, and I don't think the others, either, would ever have attacked her tool, her means of a livelihood."

The stenographer—in an effort to protect her machine from physical damage—lifted her machine, holding it tightly to her chest with one arm, and flailing the other outward "in the only gesture of violence . . . that I observed throughout the course of the events," Jane later said.

The stenotype—the tape that held the official record of the meeting—slid out, spreading across the floor.

Senator Toth had had enough. *Arrest that woman! Arrest that woman!* he shouted to the police.

Officer McGovern, one of the officers on duty, responded—not by arresting Jane, but by asking her to remove herself by taking a seat in a chair on the stage.

Jane watched the scene unfold before her. Protestors swooped in, gathering up the tape and tossing it in the air in silence, like a surreal piece of performance art. The *Post* reported a different version than Jane's recollection. The paper reported that protestors were actively destroying the record, ripping the tape to shreds with glee.

"I often didn't know what to do," Janc once said about her many battles with the city and Moses. "[I] only escaped mistakes by the skin of my teeth, and learned as I went along, mostly from other people who were a lot better informed about one thing or another than I was."

But her informal, self-taught education in activism led her, in many ways, to this very moment. *Something had to end this*, Jane thought. She rose again, marching back down to the floor, despite the officer's insistence that she remain seated and silent.

Jane took the mic. *There is no hearing because the record is gone*, she told them all. *And without a record, there can't be a hearing.*

It's over.

You're over.

* * *

After a decade of public battles, grassroots organizing, protests, and political action, the infamous Seward Park hearing was deemed invalid. The approval process would be delayed. More people would speak up, in outcry. Public officials would be swayed, one by one.

Eventually, the project would be scrapped altogether.

Jane and her fellow organizers took on Robert Moses

(again) . . . and won. In a confetti swirl of steno-tape, no less.

Downtown Manhattan was spared from the clutches of urban renewal, but Jane Jacobs's fight wasn't over. Not yet. Her public act of civil disobedience really ruffled feathers, and her stunt came with a cost. Minutes after the hearing broke apart, as Jane and protestors filed out, the police captain tapped her on the shoulder.

Tapped.

Tapped?

Let's pause here while we're celebrating a culminating victory. Jane's a white, middle-age lady disrupting a public hearing in the 1960s. What is the likelihood of a police officer gently *tapping* a Black activist in 1968? Or today?

Just five years earlier, on May 3, 1963, a white commissioner ordered police to club, attack, and use power hoses on Black children in Birmingham, Alabama. Police used nightsticks on Black children for protesting. The children were marching for civil rights: equal rights for everyone.

This is just one snapshot of many of America's brutal response to Black people organizing for equal rights—for engaging in protest and direct action, like Jane and the residents of the West Village did. "We can never be satisfied as long as the Negro is the victim of the unspeakable horrors of police brutality," Martin Luther King said in his famous 'I Have a Dream' speech, just one month after the Children's Crusade in Birmingham.

Jane was *tapped*. A fumbling officer squeaked out his orders: *You're under arrest*, he told her.

The truth is, her arrest was ridiculous. She should have received a handshake, not a jail cell. Still, her treatment was also an example of her relative privilege as a white organizer—and of biased policing in general.

The cop handcuffed Jane while she asked, "What's the charge? Why am I being arrested?" But no one could really say why, not even the police captain, who *actually apologized* as he arrested her.

Jane was the only protestor who was hauled off to the seventh precinct police station. She was booked with disorderly conduct charges. "I couldn't be arrested in a better cause," she told the *New York Post*. Decades later, she admitted that she "enjoyed the ride in the patrol wagon."

The crowd outside the station house chanted again: "We want Jane! We want Jane!"

When she was released two hours later, she was by no means off the hook. Just one week later, Jane appeared in court. The initial charge of disorderly conduct morphed into four separate, startlingly severe felony charges, including criminal riot.

There was no way she was pleading guilty. The charges "bear no relation to what happened," Jane told reporters.

Jane Jacobs was now facing up to four years in prison.

For standing up and doing the right thing.

CHAPTER 12

LEAVING AMERICA

"I'm glad I was brought up an American, but I'm not
cut out to be a citizen of an empire."

—JANE JACOBS[1]

After her arrest, Jane was considered a hero to many New
Yorkers, who were appalled by the reports in the papers.
The prosecution "made out what a dangerous character I
was: inciting to riot," Jane said about the unjust charges she
faced. "I was a menace on the streets. I had to be silenced."

The newspapers took to her cause, reporting on the
groundswell of outrage around the criminal charges. Her
friends held fundraisers to cover her attorney fees, which
were racking up. (Her lawyer's strategy was to drag the
thing out to give the other side time to cool their hysteria.)

Public sentiment likely played a role in the outcome
of the court's decision: the felony charges were eventually
reduced to a single charge of disorderly conduct, to which
Jane pleaded guilty. The judge went easy on a woman who
was simply exercising her freedom of speech.

She was finally free.

* * *

The federal government came down with their verdict: the plans for Lomex were environmentally unacceptable; the pollution would be oppressive, harmful, and irreversible. By 1969, Mayor Lindsay came out against the project, officially withdrawing his support. The US government, growing uncomfortable with all of the bad press, wanted to put this thing to rest too. By 1972, Moses's plan for New York was de-mapped, once and for all. What might have looked like an overnight success to outsiders was ten—or thirty, or sixty—years in the making, depending on where you drew the starting line.

Lomex was (finally) dead, and urban renewal was deemed toxic.

Alongside her neighbors, Jane had spent years championing people's basic rights. The ongoing fight had disrupted her sleep, her work, and her family. "I resent, to tell you the truth," she told *Vogue* magazine, "the time I've had to spend on these civic battles."

Even with strict boundaries in place around her writing time (her daughter once screened a phone call from Mayor Lindsay himself, telling him that her mother was unavailable for conversation until after 4:00 p.m.), Jane felt the exhaustion from a decade of juggling parenting with work and activism:

"It's a terrible imposition when the city threatens its citizens in such a way that they can't finish their work. Why, I know artists who aren't getting their pictures painted because of an expressway, poets who aren't getting their poems done."

Still, she believed it was all necessary. And remarkably, in defiance of all odds, the people won.

But when that final verdict came in, Jane Jacobs wasn't around to celebrate. She had already moved on.

By then, "the fight, the actual fight, was carried on by other people—the fight that finally put that expressway to rest," Jane said. "So that will have to be the tale of someone else, how that was done."

* * *

Jane Jacobs had been jailed before. The unconventional and intellectual fifty-one-year-old mother of three was first arrested back in December 1967, months before she was hauled off in a cop car at the Lomex hearing.

Her first arrest had nothing at all to do with a highway, or with Robert Moses. It had to do with something that was thousands of miles away and at the same time far more destructive than any outside force that Jane had ever battled. The United States was at war with Vietnam, and her boys, now young adults, were facing a draft.

The war in Vietnam was a catastrophe. By the end of the war, three million people (including fifty-eight thou-

Jane, Bob, and daughter Mary at peace march, 1967. FRED W. MCDARRAH/GETTY

sand Americans) had died. The United States said they got involved to stop the spread of communism. But America had economic interests in the region. Regular people saw through the lies and knew the war was about money. The images and stories of brutality against the Vietnamese people, including children and the elderly, were haunting. Many Americans, like Jane, were opposed to the staggering loss of life that was happening overseas.

As in her public battles with Moses, City Hall, politicians, and developers, Jane spent most of 1967 fighting

American National Guards defending the Pentagon building at the Anti-Vietnam Peace March, Arlington, Virginia, USA. Oct 21st, 1967. MARC RIBOUD/MAGNUM

against the US government's decision to wage war. Jane's kind of fighting, that is—protesting, disrupting, and speaking up.

She took her daughter to a peace march at the UN. She published an ad in the *New York Post* and the *New York Review of Books*, cosigning a statement along with James Baldwin, Norman Mailer, Susan Sontag, and others decrying the war and asserting their refusal to pay a tax increase to fund the war effort. (The *New York Times* and the *Washington Post* refused to publish their statement.)

And then she went to Washington.

It was the March on the Pentagon of October 1967. The air was unseasonably warm, and young people were out in droves in Washington, marching for peace. There had never been an antiwar protest of this magnitude before. Fifty thousand people gathered at Lincoln Memorial, listened to Peter, Paul and Mary sing songs of collaboration and resistance, and marched to the Pentagon. Jane Jacobs joined the crowd as a fifty-one-year-old with adult children of her own.

"Vietnam demands disobedience," she wrote around this time. "Civil disobedience affirms that outside the corridors of power are men and women who make judgments, possess courage, form intentions, captain their souls, and act on their own." To Jane, the war was obviously wrong. She felt that it was her moral duty to speak out against her government.

But something else happened when she joined marches and picket lines. Her act of protest revealed a deeper understanding of military power.

The United States government had come prepared. The National Guard wielded bayonets. Faceless men in gas masks readied themselves as if they were marching into a battlefield. Helicopters circled above; armored tanks took their positions.

Some protestors tried to run through the armed soldiers. Others damaged property and fencing. The National Guard responded by arresting hundreds of people—ordinary people practicing their right to express dissent and disgust, who were caught in the crossfire and hauled off into vans.

"I was outraged that they should be marching on me, on me, an American!" Jane later said.

Jane's epiphany on America's militarized police force wasn't a groundbreaking observation—and it's a naïve comment, considering the way American policing shaped the very cities she dedicated her life to. But in March of 1967, something shifted.

It was the day that marked the beginning of the end of Jane Jacobs as a proud, patriotic citizen of the United States.

* * *

Two months after the March on Washington, Jane attended a high-profile protest in New York City. It was all rather tame: the big idea was simply to sit down on the sidewalk.

There was nothing violent about it.

She and hundreds of others sat outside the Whitehall Induction Center in New York City to block the entrance of the building where the US army kept offices and records of the young men who were being drafted into the war.

Over 250 people were arrested at the anti-draft protest that day in December 1967. Jane was imprisoned alongside Susan Sontag, Grace Paley, Allen Ginsburg, and Dr. Benjamin Spock, other writers and public figures who were using their celebrity to bring attention to the cause.

Jane had just penned a letter to the *New York Times*, disgusted with the United States government: "We have proceeded for the past two and a half years to engage in an enterprise sicker and uglier than war itself: an enterprise of slaughtering, starving, destroying and uprooting, to no purpose except to postpone acknowledging failure. This is now the only point of our presence in Vietnam."

The snapshot of Jane in jail shows her composed, patient, and knowing face. She sits sphinxlike, as if she had all the time in the world.

Was she relieved?

Perhaps.

By then, she had likely decided her next move.

* * *

"You know, we didn't raise these boys to go to jail," Bob said to Jane.

But that's exactly where the boys were headed if they refused the draft.

Jane was willing to accept arrest and jail time as the consequence for her dissent. But she would never make the ultimate, and in her opinion unnecessary, sacrifice. She would not risk her sons' lives for a war that she was completely against.

* * *

In 1968, with her sons James and Edward approaching draft age, Jane and her family moved to the city of Toronto, Canada, in protest of the war. Sometimes resistance means staying put and not backing down. Other times, it looks like walking away.

This was not a huge internal conflict for Jane. Instead, it was a clear path forward. And it had everything to do with what had just gone down in Washington. It had everything to do with the feeling that overtook her—that *she* was the enemy on the very soil of the land she called home. "I fell out of love with my country. It sounds ridiculous, but I didn't feel a part of America anymore."

CHAPTER 13

TYPICAL JANE

". . . we need unlimited independent thinkers with
unlimited skepticism and curiosity."

—JANE JACOBS[1]

The emotional lady with hurt feelings moved to Canada,
ran a feature article in *New York Magazine* in 1969. The
reporter, Peter Blake, described the Jacobses' move as an
"overreaction" to the criminal charges Jane faced after the
Lomex hearing. "She was alleged to have smashed [the
stenotype machine] in a fit," he wrote, assuming that Jane's
border-crossing was due to some inability to control her
emotions around her punishment.

"I wasn't leaving Greenwich Village for Toronto," Jane said
about her decision. "I was leaving the United States for Canada.
And it was because of the Vietnam War, which neither Greenwich Village nor Toronto had anything to do with instigating."

Once in Toronto with her husband, two sons, and
daughter, Jane felt exhilarated. They were starting anew in
their second act, a revival of her early days in New York City.

"I find it almost too exciting," Jane wrote in the Canadian newspaper *Globe and Mail*, a year after her move. "Here is the most hopeful and healthy city in North America, still untangled, still with options." Jane was once again curious and eager for this new chapter in her life, and for a vibrant, bustling city to explore.

* * *

A few months after their arrival, the Jacobses purchased a house around the corner from their rented home in the Annex, a district near the University of Toronto where many students and professors lived. Jane—the writer who was fixated on what makes a place flourish—filled her hands with mulberries, chestnuts, pears, and apples from one backyard, transporting them to their new garden. The Jacobses were planting new seeds in the place they'd call home for the remainder of their lives. "It was an adventure, and we were all together," Jane said.

Her friends in New York were incredulous. *Well, when are you coming back?* they would ask her. It was typical American self-centeredness, Jane thought of her friends' push for the Jacobses to return to the "real world": "One of the . . . sins of Americans is that they don't seem to think that any place outside the United States is totally real; their curiosity about Canada seems almost non-existent."

Jane didn't hate everything about America. She loved her

family and friends there, and her life in the Village. (Even her decision to become a Canadian citizen was a practical matter: she simply wanted to vote in Canadian elections.)

Leaving America didn't feel like a defeat.

In fact, it felt like the very opposite: an unexpected treasure that life revealed to her.

It was a gift.

* * *

Today, Jane Jacobs is known for her lasting impact on cities and urbanism, and for her grassroots organizing against one of the most powerful men in New York.

Death and Life has secured a place in the canon of texts on city building and planning—warranted criticisms and all. It was a phenomenon she found surprising, crediting a generation of young people in particular who embraced and spread her ideas.

Jane never imagined that her impact on culture would be so profound. She looked at her own work as having been most impactful in the field of economics—*not* urbanism or activism.

The succession of books that followed her best known work had less to do with cities, instead gravitating toward the question: "What makes economic expansion happen?" She hints at this at the end of *Death and Life*. And she goes even deeper into this idea in her later books—*The Nature of Economies* and *The Economy of Cities*.

"I was interested in process, not in the notion that you can wave a wand and control things and get some end result," Jane said, looking back on her body of work. "I just want to know how to keep the life going, which in my mind is the purpose of life."

To Jane, her ideas on how a place expands and grows economically were the great theme of her life's work. "And if I am thought of as a great thinker, that will be why."

Jane's last book, *Dark Age Ahead*, was published in 2004, two years before her death. The topic was broader in scope and loftier than that of her previous works. It was a warning and a rallying cry to the dangers that face our democracy in the twenty-first century.

Despite the ominous title, *Dark Age Ahead* was a work of optimism and hope. She argued that we have so much more work to do in order to create thriving communities and to preserve the health of democracy as we know it. Government needs to be both responsive and responsible, working in concert with citizens.

She anticipated our current housing crisis in her final work too. Lack of housing and the high costs of housing are failures of our government, she argued. Governments have a responsibility to make it possible and easy to build more homes, and to regulate the skyrocketing costs of housing—which shouldn't be an investment in our portfolio but a human right.

* * *

Jane's life story has been distorted into a kind of sainthood, Peter Laurence argues, with Jane as a mythic woman who is not quite of this world. At once rebellious, brilliant, and impatient, writes Adam Gopnik, Jane Jacobs is like a modern-day Joan of Arc, the teenage girl who led an entire French army to victory.

She's "the mother of all preservations, pedestrians, and community activists," writes *City Journal*, noting her influence on everyone from niche professionals to radical political organizers and the ordinary people walking down a sidewalk.

To some, Jane was an all-knowing sage with a "radiant aura." To others, she was the overprepared den mother, ready with her bag full of tricks and teachable moments.

Jane wanted *nothing* to do with the fandom or caricatures of her as a leader of a movement. "I don't want disciples," she said. "My knowledge and talents are much too skimpy. The last thing I would want is to inadvertently limit other people with minds of their own."

* * *

Jane believed that people without titles or power are capable of significant, transformative things—that their lived experiences are valuable and matter far more than the theories of so-called experts, who hated cities and tried to erase them. "I'm always amazed at how many people don't trust their own experience," she told an interviewer. "They don't think that what happened to them can be important." The worst thing would be to follow a prescription for how to do something without thinking critically about it—especially if that prescription originated outside a community, and not by the people who lived there.

If Jane had any rules for other people, they would be, simply, to think for oneself, and to value one's own inherent worth. "I would like it to be understood, and increasingly understood as time passes, that all our human economic achievements have been done by ordinary people, not by exceptionally educated people, or by elites, or by supernatural forces, for heaven's sake. Yet without understanding this, people are all too willing to fall for the idea that they can't do this, they themselves, or anybody they know, because they're too ordinary."

* * *

Jane Jacobs died in Toronto at the age of eighty-nine, a decade after her husband Bob's death, and two years after the publication of her final book. She had relished sticking around long enough to see how (some) things turned out. "My only regret is that the human span is so limited," she admitted. "I'm just so curious to see what happens."

Toward the end of her life, Jane worked with Barbara Hall, the mayor of Toronto, advising her on a declining industrial historic neighborhood. (Jane's prescription was to mix the uses to allow for both homes *and* commerce.) Mayor Hall remembers Jane's voice, urging her above all else to be brave and bold.

Her first few years in Toronto were quiet, though. After decades of committee meetings and campaign-building in New York City, she purposefully avoided taking part in community organizing.

Instead, Jane laid low. She preferred her writing desk and the feelings of security that came with everyday life as a homebody: garden-tending, chain-smoking, chain-sipping (beer or vermouth), baking bread, making jam, and playing jigsaw puzzles, to name a few of her favorite pastimes. She turned down interviews, speaking engagements, and rarely made commitments outside the home. It was time to embrace life on her own terms.

Jane was especially looking forward to taking a break from the grueling, long hours of political organizing to focus on her life's work: writing books. She returned to a strict schedule of writing, keeping the hours between 9:30 a.m. and 4:00 p.m. as her uninterrupted work time. "If the chores aren't done by 9:30 they remain undone. The beds, the marketing, whatever," she explained.

But her break from activism didn't last long. Toronto was facing its very own battle with developers and city government. The Spadina Expressway, an urban highway, had been snaking its way through the city for years and now it was coming for the very street of their first rented flat—threatening homes, parks, and livelihoods.

There was, of course, no way that she would remain an onlooker.

There was far too much work to do.

In a letter to her mother in 1972, Jane talked about the "hated villains" who were trying, like Moses, to push a highway through her neighborhood. It was déjà vu. But Jane knew from experience that the Canadian citizen effort to stop the expressway was working, and the powers that be had a huge uphill battle ahead. "My rule of thumb is that an Expressway has to be killed three times before it is dead," she wrote, "so this one has only one more life to go and I am pretty confident it won't make it, as long as we have such good fighters on our side, which we do."

It was typical Jane.

From her initial foray into organizing to keep the storied Washington Square Park as a place for people, not cars; to leading the effort against a developer who wanted to bulldoze fourteen blocks of the West Village; to working with seven hundred community members to build over four hundred affordable apartments in her downtown New York neighborhood; to the culminating, final blow to urban renewal—her grassroots, sustained effort against the dystopian Lomex that would have decimated the Lower

Manhattan neighborhoods of Chinatown, Little Italy, and SoHo—Jane found herself in a battle for her neighborhood, yet again.

Was it a great burden on her time?

Yes.

She *said* she resented the nuisance.

But did she *completely* detest the collaborative late nights, creative scheming, and collective buzz of people determining their own futures?

Could Jane imagine doing it any other way?

Not at all.

The Spadina Expressway never did get completed, thanks to the advocacy and political lobbying that Jane took part in but decidedly did *not* lead. She admitted to having a "bang-up good time in the process" and enjoying the "satisfying vengeance against the rascals in the end."

This was Jane from the Village, now working alongside her Toronto neighbors.

It was a new fight, but it was also the same old fight.

Together, they flexed their problem-solving powers as a collaborative, responsive force to be reckoned with.

They were mothers, housewives, journalists, architects, writers, students, professors, artists, and carpenters. They were shopkeepers, professors, immigrants, and children.

They were ordinary people. And they won.

(Again.)

RESEARCHING THIS BOOK

Jane wasn't into the idea of a biography. (*I know . . . right?*)
She *did* willingly collaborate with Peter Laurence toward
the end of her life—a biographer whose work I have relied
on throughout my research process, along with Robert
Kanigel. But, for the most part, she stayed away from
people who wished to delve into her psyche and reveal deep
insights about her personal life or character.

I'll make a not-so-wild guess as to *why* she was so hesi-
tant to participate in TV interviews or biographical studies:
Jane was never the hero. She never wanted to be and refuted
such a characterization. It was always about the collective
power of so-called ordinary people.

For Jane, it was always about *you.*

Your potential.

Your power.

My research process began with a deep dive into primary
sources—which is basically another way of saying that I
read Jane's own words—her books, her oral interviews, her
writings, and her letters.

I spent time with Jane's archive at the Burns Library at
Boston College, in the digitized collections of the Rockefeller Archive Center, and with the oral history collections

at the Greenwich Village Society of Historic Preservation.

The book *Ideas That Matter*, edited by Max Allen and first published in Ontario by Ginger Press in 1997, is a treasure trove of primary sources that proved to be invaluable throughout my research process. It includes Jane's autobiography, news clippings of the media storm after the publication of *Death and Life*, personal letters, and Jane's full response to a US government interrogation.

In addition to her published books, *Vital Little Plans* (edited by Samuel Zipp and Nathan Storring) is a collection of Jane's articles and essays. It was enormously helpful to consult all of her shorter works in one place, along with Zipp and Storring's thoughtful analysis.

SOME BOOKS, VIDEOS, AND WEBSITES I RECOMMEND

By Jane

Dark Age Ahead (Random House, 2004)
The Nature of Economies (Modern Library, 2000)
A Schoolteacher in Old Alaska: The Story of Hannah Breece (Random House, 1995)
Systems of Survival: A Dialogue on the Moral Foundations of Commerce and Politics (Random House, 1992)
Cities and the Wealth of Nations: Principles of Economic Life (Random House, 1984)
The Question of Separatism: Quebec and the Struggle over Sovereignty (Random House, 1980)
The Economy of Cities (Random House, 1969)
The Death and Life of Great American Cities (Random House, 1961)
The Girl on the Hat (for children) (Oxford University Press, 1990)

About Jane

Allen, Max, ed. *Ideas That Matter: The Worlds of Jane Jacobs*. Owen Sound, Ontario: Ginger Press, 1997; rev. ed. Washington, DC: Island Press, 2011.

Center for the Living City. "Jane Jacobs and the Center." Center for the Living City website, 2022. https://centerforthelivingcity.org/janejacobs.

Flint, Anthony. *Wrestling with Moses*. New York: Random House Trade Paperbacks, 2011.

Jacobs, Jane. *Oral History Interview Conducted for Greenwich Village Society for Historic Preservation*. Interview with Leticia Kent. Toronto, Canada: October 1997.

Jacobs, Jane. *Vital Little Plans*. Edited by Nathan Storring and Samuel Zipp. New York: Random House, 2016.

Jane Jacobs: The Last Interview and Other Conversations. Brooklyn: Melville House Publishing, 2016.

Jane's Walk. Official website. 2022. https://janeswalk.org/.

Kanigel, Robert. *Eyes on the Street: The Life of Jane Jacobs*. New York: Alfred A. Knopf, 2016.

Laurence, Peter L. *Becoming Jane Jacobs*. Philadelphia: University of Pennsylvania Press, 2016.

Tyrnauer, Matt, dir. *Citizen Jane: Battle for the City*. Orland Park, Illinois: MPI Media Group, 2016.

Beyond Jane

Digital Scholarship Lab. "The Mapping Inequality Project." The University of Richmond, 2022. https://dsl.richmond.edu/panorama/redlining/.

"Housing Segregation Is Everything." *Code Switch*, NPR, April 11, 2018. https://www.npr.org/sections/codeswitch/2018/04/11/601494521/video-housing-segregation-in-everything.

Reynolds, Jason and Ibram X. Kendi. *Stamped: Racism, Antiracism, and You*. New York: Little, Brown and Company, 2020.

Rothstein, Richard. *The Color of Law: A Forgotten History of How Our Government Segregated America*. New York, London: Liveright Publishing Corporation, 2017.

Southern Poverty Law Center, Teaching Tolerance. "Webinar on the book *The Color of Law*." *Learning for Justice* website, November 5, 2019. https://www.learningforjustice.org/professional-development/webinars/the-color-of-law.

Zinn, Howard. *A Young People's History of the United States: Revised and Updated*. Adapted by Rebecca Stefoff; contributions by Ed Morales. New York: Seven Stories Press, 2022.

NOTES

Key to Abbreviations in the Notes

Archives

Burns Library—Jane Jacobs Papers, MS.1995.029, 1860–2006 (bulk 1960–2002), Burns Library, Boston College, Boston, Massachusetts

Rockefeller—Downtown-Lower Manhattan Association, Inc. records (FA085), Rockefeller Archive Center, Sleepy Hollow, New York

Kent, GVHSP—Jane Jacobs. *Oral History Interview Conducted for Greenwich Village Society for Historic Preservation*, interview by Leticia Kent, Toronto, Canada: October 1997.

Books by Jane Jacobs

Death and Life—Jane Jacobs, *The Death and Life of Great American Cities* (New York: Random House, 1961).

Other Books

Eyes on the Street—Robert Kanigel, *Eyes on the Street* (New York: Alfred A. Knopf, 2016).

Ideas That Matter—Max Allen, ed., *Ideas That Matter* (Owen Sound, Ontario: Ginger Press, 1997).

Last Interview—*Jane Jacobs: The Last Interview and Other Conversations* (Brooklyn: Melville House Publishing, 2016).

Vital Little Plans—Jacobs, Jane, *Vital Little Plans*, ed. Samuel Zipp and Nathan Storring (New York: Random House, 2016).

* * *

Introduction

1. Hank Bromley, "The Convention Follies, Part 5: A Conversation with Jane Jacobs," *Artvoice* 11, no. 30 (July 27, 2000).
2. Burns, Jane Jacobs to Stewart Brand, January 31, 1994.
3. Death and Life, illustration note.

Philadelphia, 1955

1. Vital Little Plans, p. 51.

Chapter 1

1. Eyes on the Street, p. 46.

Chapter 2

1. Death and Life, pp. 50–52.

Chapter 3

1. Last Interview, p. 12.
2. Howard Zinn, "Another McCarthy Era," interview by Steven Rosenfeld, December 2, 2003, https://www.howardzinn.org/another-mccarthy-era/.

Chapter 4

1. Ideas That Matter, pp. 25–27.
2. Richard Rothstein, *The Color of Law: A Forgotten History of How Our Government Segregated America* (New York, London: Liveright Publishing Corporation, 2017) p. xiv.

Chapter 5

1. Last Interview, p. 18.
2. Eyes on the Street, p. 134.

Chapter 6

1. Death and Life, p. 338.
2. Ideas That Matter, p. 131.
3. George Lakey, *How We Win: A Guide to Nonviolent Direct Action Campaigning* (Brooklyn: Melville House Publishing, 2018) p. 3.

Chapter 7

1. Death and Life, p. 238.
2. "I do not entertain . . .," "We are copying failure," and "attempt to make"— Jane Jacobs, "Letter from Jane Jacobs to Chadbourne Gilpatric, 1959 July 23," 100 Years: The Rockefeller Foundation, accessed February 28, 2020, https://rockfound.rockarch.org/digital-library-listing/-/asset_publisher/yYxpQfeI-4W8N/content/letter-from-jane-jacobs-to-chadbourne-gilpatric-1959-july-23.
3. William H. Whyte, cover endorsement, Death and Life.
4. Death and Life, p. 84.
5. Leticia Kent, "Against Urban Renewal, for Urban Life," *New York Times*, May 25, 1969.
6. Angela Davis, *Freedom Is a Constant Struggle: Ferguson, Palestine, and the Foundations of a Movement* (Chicago: Haymarket Books, 2016) pp. 64–65.

7. Kendi, Ibram X. Introduction to *Stamped: Racism, Antiracism, and You* by Jason Reynolds and Ibram X. Kendi (New York: Little, Brown and Company, 2020) pp. xi-xii.

8. Amina Yasin, "Whose Streets? Black Streets," *The Tyee*, June 18, 2020, https://thetyee.ca/analysis/2020/06/18/whose-streets-black-streets/.

9. Ta-Nehisi Coates, *We Were Eight Years in Power: An American Tragedy* (New York: One World Publications, 2017).

10. Ideas That Matter, pp. 83-85.

Chapter 8

1. Ideas that Matter, pp. 25-27.
2. Vital Little Plans, p. 223.
3. Eyes on the Street, pp. 220-223.
4. Kent, "Against Urban Renewal."
5. Eyes on the Street, p. 222.
6. Bromley, "The Convention Follies."
7. Burns, Robert Moses to Bennett Cerf, November 15, 1961.
8. Burns, General correspondence from Jane Jacobs, 2002-2004, Box 43, Folder 9. Letter from Mumford to Jacobs, June 18, 1958.
9. Ideas That Matter, p. 96.

Chapter 9

1. Vital Little Plans, p. 45.

Chapter 10

1. Vital Little Plans, p. 204.
2. Death and Life, p. 15.

Chapter 11

1. Last Interview, pp. 45-46.

Chapter 12

1. Duneier, Mitchell. "The Way We Live Now: Questions for Jane Jacobs," *New York Times*, April 9, 2000, https://nyti.ms/2EdqCIt.

Chapter 13

1. Vital Little Plans, pp. 455–459.

IMAGE CREDITS

PAGE 4: Jane Jacobs in 1969. Copyright © Elliott Erwitt / Magnum PhotosTEST 01-Stock (Photogs).

PAGE 34: Christopher St. & Bleecker St., 1936. Courtesy of the New York Public Library.

PAGE 86: Housing development in East Harlem. A similar photo of East Harlem housing was included in Jane's article in Architectural Forum (a version of her Harvard speech) in June 1956. Courtesy of the Municipal Archives, City of New York.

PAGE 99: Jane on her bicycle, Washington Street, 1963. Courtesy of Getty, by Bob Gomel.

PAGE 119: Save the Square! Poster documenting the fight to close Washington Square to vehicle traffic in the 1950s. Poster by Weiner, Pickwick Offset Press; Shirley Hayes Papers, New-York Historical Society Library, 80479d. Photograph © New-York Historical Society.

PAGE 123: Jane protesting at PS41, 1964. Courtesy of Getty, by Fred W. McDarrah.

PAGE 145: Jane Jacobs, center, at the White Horse Tavern on Hudson Street in Greenwich Village, 1961. Copyright © 2018 Cervin Robinson, cerv_rob@yahoo.com.

PAGE 196: Jane Jacobs holding up documents at a press conference of the Committee to Save the West Village, Lions Head Restaurant, 1961. Courtesy of the New York World-Telegram and Sun Newspaper Photograph Collection, Library of Congress, by Phil Stanziola.

PAGE 234: Jane, Bob, and daughter Mary at peace march, 1967. Courtesy of Getty, by Fred W. McDarrah.

PAGE 235: American National Guards defending the Pentagon building at the Anti-Vietnam Peace March, Arlington, Virginia, Oct 21, 1967. Copyright © Marc Riboud / Fonds Marc Riboud au MNAAG / Magnum PhotosTEST 02-Stock (Estate).

ACKNOWLEDGMENTS

I'd like to extend my sincere gratitude to the people who helped with this book. Thank you to my editors, Lauren Hooker and Tal Mancini, and my agent, Bibi Lewis, my coconspirators (in the best way possible!), who believed in this project from the very beginning and pushed me to engage deeply with Jane's story and legacy.

There are people who helped me and probably don't know that they did. Thank you to the urbanists, activists, scholars, writers, and practitioners who informed my thinking about placemaking, citizen-organizing, and city-building today. I'd also like to thank the historians, biographers, and archivists who informed my understanding of Jane's ideas and life's work of relentless activism.

There were a few teachers I had the good fortune to learn from. Thank you to the educators who planted the seed of possibility that it might be worth it to take my writing work seriously: Ms. Bernice Nicolari at Shelton High School, Professor Naomi Miller at Boston University, and Professor Donna Weber at Simmons University.

I would like to thank my dear family and friends; especially my parents Mary and Richard Robbins, my sister Megan, my daughter Sophie, son Sebastian, niece Elizah, and my devoted husband Eugene, who coparented with me during a pandemic while I wrote this book.

My reading interests and writing work have always circled back to nonfiction feminist stories rooted in the past. I must, of course, thank Jane Jacobs, whose book, *Death and Life*, was an inspiration to me first as a young person in Boston in 1998 as I watched "The Big Dig" unfold before my very eyes in my new city. This was the most expensive construction project in US history to date and its aim was to reverse the damage of the freeways that had carved through downtown neighborhoods by sinking them underground, away from people. Watching this massive, costly effort while reading Jane's takedown of the conventional building wisdom of the time was an eye-opening experience for me.

When I started writing this book, I felt pretty confident that I wanted to tell young readers all about the harms and legacy of urban renewal. (Oh, there's some of that here, yes.) But research yields unexpected journeys—instead, the story of Jane's relentless, disciplined, and principled activism surfaced. Struck by her intuitive and sometimes improvisational sixth sense for inverting the power struc-ture, I became captivated by Jane's ability to weave a web of connections and influence bigger than any one person.

It's my hope that you, too, have been wowed by Jane Jacobs and—perhaps more importantly—are inspired by the collective power of ordinary people who are in fact the experts of their own lived experiences.

Writing for young readers has been one of the great privileges of my creative life. My sincere gratitude and appreciation to you, my reader.

INDEX

mixed-use housing developed
by, 74

Lakey, George, 113
LaMountain, Gerard, 214–15, 218,
    221
Landmarks Preservation Law, in
    New York City, 216
"Last Car Thru," 126
Laurence, Peter, 131, 169–70, 245
Le Corbusier, 91, 138–40
Lincoln Center, 98
    as development project, 96–97
    displacement of minorities for,
        96–97
    Jacobs, Jane, criticism of, 107
Lindsay, John, 219
"Listen, Robert Moses" (Dylan), 217
Logue, Ed, 72–73, 77
Lomex. *See* Lower Manhattan
    Expressway
Long Island Expressway, 98
Lower Manhattan Expressway
    (Lomex), 210, 213, 222
    City Planning Commission, 212
    Joint Committee to Stop
        the Lower Manhattan
        Expressway, 215–19
    LaMountain and, 214–15, 218, 221
    in media, 220

neighborhood demolition as part
    of, 212
public hearings on, 219
public opposition to, 232
public support for, 224
scrapping of, 232
Lynch, Kevin, 166
Lynch, Nancy, 164
Lyons, Edith, 109–11, 184

Mademoiselle, 164
Mailer, Norman, 235
March on the Pentagon, 236
Martin, Trayvon, 153
Marx, Karl, 56
McCarthy, Joseph, 56–57
McCarthyism, 56–57. *See also*
    communism
Mead, Margaret, 126
Metropolitan Opera, 96–97
mixed-use housing, in Harlem
    neighborhood, 74–75
modernism movement, 135–36
    city planning and, 138–39
Moholy-Nagy, László, 136
Moses, Robert. *See also* Jacobs,
    Jane; Washington Square Park;
    specific projects
    catholic church and, 221–22
    corruptness of, 103

WHAT'S NEXT?

How can *you* make a difference in your community? To apply some of the ideas you've learned here to your village, town, or city, visit www.rebeccaapitts.com/myplace for guides for young people and educators.

FOR THE ADULT READERS

Are you a teacher, educator, librarian, parent, inspirational auntie or uncle, or champion of young people? Thank you for sharing this book with a young reader in your life. Please drop me a line at www.rebeccaapitts.com/janebook and let me know how I can support your classroom, library, or family discussions.